The Indomitable Mrs. Trollope

by

EILEEN BIGLAND

1954

J. B. LIPPINCOTT COMPANY

PHILADELPHIA AND NEW YORK

COPYRIGHT, 1953, BY
EILEEN BIGLAND

PRINTED IN THE
UNITED STATES OF AMERICA

FIRST IMPRESSION

Library of Congress Catalog Card Number 54-6102

To
Jonathan Curling

Acknowledgment

THE Bibliography is reproduced by kind permission of Mr. Michael Sadleir and Messrs. Constable & Co. Ltd.

Contents

THE INDOMITABLE MRS. TROLLOPE

THE TROLLOPE FAMILY

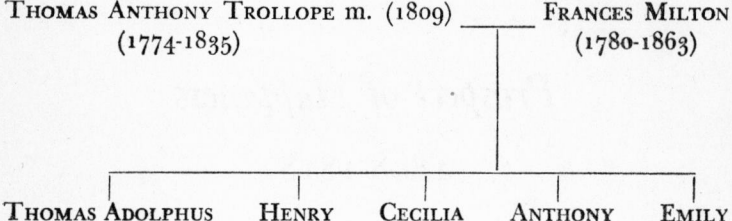

Thomas Anthony Trollope m. (1809) ——— Frances Milton
(1774-1835)   (1780-1863)

| Thomas Adolphus | Henry | Cecilia | Anthony | Emily |

1

Prospect of Happiness
1808-1818

(*i*)

ON A late October day in 1808 a young woman sat at a writing-desk in the drawing-room of Heckfield Vicarage near Reading, alternately gazing out of the window and nibbling the tip of her quill pen. Presently she frowned, straightened her slim back, and drew a sheet of paper towards her. Her mind was made up—why should she, normally a creature of impulse, have hesitated in this stupid fashion? She began to write swiftly in a fine, sloping hand:

> It does not require three weeks' consideration, Mr. Trollope, to enable me to tell you that the letter you left with me last night was most flattering and gratifying to me. I value your good opinion too highly not to feel that the generous proof you have given me of it must for ever, and in any event, be remembered by me with pride and gratitude. But I fear you are not sufficiently aware that your choice, so flattering to me, is for yourself a very imprudent one. . . .

She laid down the pen and gave a little sigh. Really, it was extraordinarily difficult to explain to the suitor whose recent visit had been so heart-stirring; yet her innate honesty told her it had to be done. He was Thomas Anthony Trollope, a renowned classical scholar who was a barrister of the Middle Temple and heir to his wealthy maternal uncle, Adolphus Meetkerke, a gentleman of aristocratic Dutch descent: she was plain Frances Milton, twenty-seven year old daughter of an impoverished and eccentric country vicar whose expensive hobby was to take out patents for mechanical inventions supposed to reduce the danger of accidents to stage-coaches, and whose father had been a saddler in Bristol. Moreover, the Reverend William Milton had remarried after the death of her mother, and since his stipend barely sufficed for their needs she would go to Mr. Trollope penniless. With a second sigh she bent again over her letter and set down, in remarkably precise fashion, all the obstacles in the way of their marriage. Her final paragraph, however, sounded a note of cautious hope:

> . . . in an affair of this kind I do not think it any disadvantage to either party that some time should elapse between the first contemplation and final decision of it. It gives each an opportunity of becoming acquainted with the other's opinion on many important points, which could not be canvassed before it was thought of, and which it would be useless to discuss after it was settled.

She sanded and sealed the letter carefully, hoping (Ah, how she hoped!) that Mr. Trollope would not spurn her because of her lack of possessions or prospects. A glance at the clock told her that the London-bound coach would pass through the village within the hour, so hurrying into the hall she took bonnet and cloak from a peg and set out to hand over the precious missive on which rested so much.

On the way to the village her mercurial spirits soared. How wonderful life was going to be! She and Mr. Trollope

would have a house in London, not too big but with a drawing-room large enough to hold all the brilliant folk she
longed to entertain—politicians, writers, painters, men of
learning, eminent divines. In this society she herself would
gain poise and confidence, find outlet for the quick wit so
unappreciated by country neighbours who thought only of
crops or pheasants. As for Mr. Trollope, her mind held
vision of him climbing rapidly to fame (aided by his loving,
energetic wife) until he reached the Woolsack.

On the way home, alas, these dizzy dreams faded. Mr.
Trollope would be so horrified by the contents of her letter
that he would rue his hasty proposal and seek a better-dow-
ered bride, or if he still protested his love his Uncle Meetkerke would cut him off with a shilling. Her own future
would be that of the vicar's spinster daughter carrying bowls
of soup to poor parishioners, helping at church bazaars, tending the house and garden. Worst of all that dreadful Napoleon Bonaparte might engulf the whole of Europe in his mad
desire for power and she, her family, and even Mr. Trollope,
might be in a far worse case than the French prisoners now
interned near by at Odiam. Her forebodings deepened as
she approached the vicarage and it was unfortunate that her
father chose the very moment she opened the gate to trundle
across the law in an amazing machine.

Frances Milton's over-wrought nerves snapped, for the
stretch of close-shaven turf had cost her many hours of labour. "Papa!" she cried angrily, "how *dare* you spoil the
grass like that?"

Her parent stopped the contraption with difficulty and
turned a benign rosy face. "But Fanny, my love, this is my
latest invention. I call it *Rotis volventibus*. You observe the
principle of traction—two wheels ten feet high joined together by crossbars set a foot or so apart. You step on each

bar in turn, thus revolving the wheels . . ." and he resumed his efforts on the gigantic treadmill.

Fanny snorted in disgust as she eyed the deep ruts on the grass. *Rotis volventibus* indeed! In a high sharp voice she trounced the Reverend William for a full five minutes. The coach-house, she said, was already cluttered up with his model coaches, all of which were out of date and useless; the garden was being ruined by his mechanical exercises; the money spent on his fads would have been better employed in providing his household with a few comforts; the patents he insisted on taking out were even less remunerative than that which legend said Charles II had granted to a sailor who stood on his head on the steeple of Salisbury Cathedral.

The tirade might have gone on longer had not the gong summoned them to luncheon. Mrs. Milton, disturbed by the tension in the atmosphere, prattled on about parish affairs while her cowed husband answered in monosyllables from the end of the table and her step-daughter sat tight-lipped and silent. Fanny was trying hard to control her temper but when the servant placed a meat plate before her she was faced with a further reminder of her father's eccentricity. It was his contention that the sound of a knife touching porcelain was a most disagreeable one to the ear. He had therefore invented a special kind of dinner-plate which had a circular depression two inches in diameter and lined with silver in its centre. On this the meat was cut up, thus avoiding the noise he disliked. Sight of the shining silver disc roused Fanny's ire once more. With a muttered excuse she pushed back her chair and fled from the room, leaving a seriously alarmed couple behind her.

What could have upset Fanny, usually so bright and gay? Mrs. Milton hoped anxiously she wasn't sickening for anything, but the Reverend William (he was still smarting under the Charles II comparison) had darker thoughts. Devoted as he was to his child he had long been aware of her headstrong nature and had done his best to curb her quick tongue, her outbursts of rebellion, because he was fearful lest she develop into one of those "modern" young women one heard of who wished for a wider field than that of the home. Now he trusted she was not harbouring any notion of refusing that charming fellow Trollope who had spoken to him so deferentially and sensibly only the day before. Such an excellent offer was not to be despised—besides Trollope, like himself, had been a Fellow of New College. What more could a father-in-law ask? Clearing his throat he began a whispered discussion with his wife, little knowing that in the room above his daughter was indulging in a fit of hysterical weeping brought on by the fear that her parent's self-induced poverty would cause Mr. Trollope to look elsewhere for a bride.

For two days an almost tangible gloom enshrouded the vicarage. Then on the evening of the second day the London coach brought no ominous letter. Instead, Thomas Anthony Trollope arrived in person. Normally a taciturn man, preternaturally old for his years, he was on this occasion positively voluble. Nothing, so he declared in a long interview with Fanny in the drawing-room, could alter his love. He did not care whether she had six thousand pounds or sixpence, he was determined they should marry as soon as possible and on his return to London on the morrow he would begin house-hunting straightaway. Swept off her feet by this display of masterfulness Fanny blushingly assented to everything he said and when they entered the dining-room at supper-time one glance at her radiant face told the Reverend William and Mrs. Milton that the betrothal was an accomplished fact.

The wedding was fixed for the following June and no

sooner had the triumphant suitor departed than Fanny and her step-mother settled down to discussion of the trousseau while the vicar, perhaps as an act of thanksgiving, forswore his idea of patenting the *Rotis volventibus* and gave his daughter a cheque far exceeding her wildest expectations. Soon the house was littered with pins and patterns among which the two women, aided by the Heckfield dressmaker, sewed furiously; then the snowy piles of household linen had to be monogrammed; then there were exciting visits to London to buy furniture and inspect the house which Thomas Anthony had taken at 16 Keppel Street, Russell Square. Never, thought Fanny ecstatically, had a girl been so blissfully happy, and extracts from her letters to her betrothed reflect the bubbling joy she experienced during those months before her marriage:

. . . The most disagreeable of created beings, Col. —— by name, by profession Sir ——'s led captain, is, while I am writing, talking in an animated strain of eloquence to Mrs. Milton, frequently seasoning his discourse with the polished phrase, "Blood and thunder, ma'am!" so if I happen to swear a little before I conclude, be so good as to believe that I am accidentally writing down what he is saying. . . .

Again she wrote of her father's intimate friend Dr. Nott, a Prebendary of Winchester:

. . . Poor dear innocent Dr. Nott! His simplicity is quite pathetic! I am really afraid that he will be taking twopence instead of two pounds from his parishioners, merely because he does not know the difference between them. I cannot help feeling a tender interest for such lamb-like innocence of the ways of this wicked world. I dare say the night I saw him at the opera, he thought he was *only* at the play, nay, perhaps believed they were performing an oratorio.

Even in those days Fanny possessed a keen critical faculty and one wonders what the reaction of another friend Dr.

Mathias, who had achieved great popularity with a book called *Pursuits of Literature,* would have been had he known that her verdict on his Italian translation of the "Echo Song" from *Comus* was "elegantly done, but is not Milton."

(*ii*)

By mid-July Fanny Milton had become Fanny Trollope and was greatly enjoying queening it over 16 Keppel Street. In the mornings when she had seen Thomas Anthony off to his chambers in Old Square, Lincoln's Inn, she rustled importantly down to the basement to interview the cook, then gave his orders for the day to the young liveried footman without whom even a modest London establishment was not complete. Later she sallied forth along Store Street to Tottenham Court Road, sometimes making small purchases but more often studying the latest fashions. Occasionally she peregrinated westwards along the Oxford Row (now Oxford Street) but seldom walking so far as the Tyburn turnpike at the corner of the Edgware Road where all vehicles had to pay toll. After luncheon she sat in state in the front drawing-room awaiting callers, of which there were plenty since most legal people lived in Bloomsbury at that time. Thomas Anthony returned for five o'clock dinner and then, if the weather was fine, took her for a stroll round Bedford or Russell Square pointing out the houses of various judges, barristers or lawyers.

Fanny did not find this decorous existence dull. A good and prudent housekeeper, she took pride in thinking out appetising meals and superintending the little housemaid, while the bustle of London streets delighted her. Besides, she regarded these first months of her marriage as a necessary training period for her career as hostess and she still thought of Thomas Anthony and herself as the ideally suited couple.

In truth they were very far from being that. They loved each other deeply but in every other respect their natures were antagonistic. He was a shy man with a strong streak of melancholy in his character; she a talkative, gregarious creature who liked nothing better than to cram her home with visitors. He suffered from some chronic internal trouble that resulted in violent headaches to relieve which he took ever-increasing doses of calomel; she enjoyed perfect health and held the robust person's mild scorn for those who complained of aches and pains. He was tall and heavily built, with a mind that moved as ponderously as his body; she was small and slight, with an amazing fund of nervous energy, a quick, darting brain, and an overwhelming faith in her ability to overcome obstacles.

It was in the autumn, on her first visit to Julians, Uncle Meetkerke's Hertfordshire estate near Royston, that Fanny felt her first misgivings about Thomas Anthony's future. Sophisticated though she imagined herself she was awed by the large pretentious house; by Aunt Meetkerke, the elderly and stately daughter of a general, who swept down to breakfast clad in a green riding-habit and spent her days riding madly round the neighbourhood; by "Mrs. Anne" (Adolphus Meetkerke's spinster sister), an apple-cheeked little lady who did the housekeeping and trit-trotted up and down stairs carrying a basket which held an enormous bunch of keys and a tattered copy of Jane Austen's *Pride and Prejudice*. But the most alarming figure was Uncle Meetkerke himself.

Fanny had met many squires at Heckfield, but none of them had resembled this burly, rough-tongued Dutchman who behaved like the ring-master in a circus. His day began punctually at 8 a.m., when he would stand on the dining-room hearthrug, prayer-book in hand, and boom at any wretched late-comer, "Five minutes late again . . . Dearly beloved brethren . . ." The prayers were read in the same raucous tones and there was no hiatus between the "Amen" and the curt order to the groom, "William, bring round the brown mare after breakfast."

Uncle Meetkerke was a tyrant of no mean order. He ruled his tenants, the magisterial bench, and the local parson—a timid bachelor named Skinner—with a rod of iron, and in church he answered the responses so loudly that nobody else's voice could be heard. If the sermon proved lengthy he bellowed out "That's enough!" and before the vicar could descend the pulpit steps he shouted, "Come to dinner, Skinner!"—an invitation which inevitably led to a monologue on the iniquities of dissenters who, he averred, ought all to be put in the stocks.

But it was in the evenings after dinner that Uncle Meetkerke was at his most terrifying. He was a rabid Tory, and while Mrs. Meetkerke slept peacefully in a chair and "Mrs. Anne" read *Pride and Prejudice* for the hundredth time, his voice thundered through the huge, drab drawing-room as he catechised Thomas Anthony on his polititcal opinions. Now Thomas Anthony held Liberal views about which he felt very strongly and had no intention of hiding them under a bushel. Perhaps because of his very shyness he was a disputatious man. Years afterwards one of his barrister colleagues told his eldest son: "Your father never came into contact with a blockhead without insisting on irrefutably demonstrating to him that he was such. And the blockhead did not like it! He was almost invariably—at least on a point of law—right. But the world differed from him in the opinion that being so gave him the right of rolling his antagonist in the dust and executing an intellectual dance of triumph on his prostrate form."

Not even the fact that he was Uncle Meetkerke's heir could restrain him from offering that gentleman proof positive of the lamentable wrongness of Tory beliefs each time a political argument was opened and this led inevitably to an explosion.

Fanny, cowering in a corner and trying vainly to arrest her husband's attention, dreaded the moment when the infuriated old squire would roar in his loudest voice, "Now my *other* nephew, John Young . . . ," for John Young was a highly prosperous lawyer disliked by the unprosperous Thomas Anthony, and a Tory to boot, and so soon as his name was introduced into the conversation both uncle and nephew abandoned all pretence at courtesy and howled imprecations at each other. The ultimate danger—that of Uncle Meetkerke disinheriting Thomas Anthony in favour of John —was always miraculously averted by "Mrs. Anne" recommending *Pride and Prejudice* in a piping voice or by Aunt Meetkerke's gurgling awakening from her slumbers, but the nightly torture preyed on Fanny's nerves to such an extent that she returned to Keppel Street in a state of exhaustion.

Thomas Anthony was extremely concerned. While he hovered around her couch in his bumbling, helpless way she wisely seized the opportunity to lecture him on the folly of thrusting his opinions down other peoples' throats and painted a grim picture of the future that would be theirs were he to antagonise Uncle Meetkerke. She added (with the modesty becoming to a young woman of her day and age) that she would shortly bear him a child. This speech had an excellent temporary effect upon Thomas Anthony. He was genuinely ashamed of having upset the wife he loved and deeply desired a son. Knowing little of women but having heard vague and awful hints of the nervous disorders suffered during pregnancy, he vowed he would keep a guard on his tongue, and throughout that winter and spring he treated her like a piece of precious china.

In truth the carrying and bearing of children affected Fanny scarcely at all—indeed over the next seven years it became a process so familiar that she paid little heed to it—and while she realised how powerful a deterrent her pregnancy was to Thomas Anthony's outbursts she grew a trifle irritated by his hovering tactics. With some asperity she said there was no reason for a man to neglect his work simply because his wife was going to have a baby; no reason either for that wife to spend her days lolling on sofas. It was high time they began to return the hospitality given them by various legal families and started to carve a niche for themselves in Bloomsbury society.

So during the next few months there was quite a coming and going at 16 Keppel Street. Fanny gave several small dinner-parties (then held at the witching hour of 5 p.m.) which involved her in much exciting preparation, for when she and her husband were alone they never used dinner-napkins, ate by the light of two tallow candles which barely illuminated the table, and sipped but a few drops of port or sherry, though decanters of these wines were always placed ceremoniously on the shining mahogany table when the cloth was removed. At dinner-parties matters were very different! The cloth was of the best white damask and the table laid with choice pieces of family silver, china and glass, while at each place was a snowy napkin fashioned into the shape of a water-lily. Light was provided by wax candles (so dreadfully extragavant at half a crown a pound!), madeira was drunk and, after the meal, a magnum of vintage port was produced for the delectation of the gentlemen.

Since these parties were intended primarily to help Thomas Anthony in his career the guests were nearly always connected with the legal world though the gregarious Fanny enjoyed playing hostess she thought privately that some of the ladies were uninteresting creatures. More to her liking were the afternoon "At Homes" she instituted, for to these she could invite a subtle mixture of old friends and new who delighted in witty and intelligent conversation. The *pièce de résistance* at these afternoons was a huge platter filled with delicious little tarts from Mr. Pidding, a Store Street pastry-cook, and these were greatly appreciated by the company. Frequent visitors were Lady Dyer, wife of General Sir Thomas Dyer; Miss Gabell, eldest daughter of the Head Master of Winchester College; Prebendary Nott—who had been tutor to Princess Charlotte and was an "elegant" Italian scholar—Miss Mitford, Mr. Macready the actor, and a General Guglielmo Pepe, at that time in political exile from Italy, who brought a number of most entertaining country-men in his train.

The General was much sought after by London hostesses and gave a considerable *cachet* to the Keppel Street parties. He was a remarkably good-looking man but his conversation consisted of an endless stream of platitudes uttered in a slow, heavy voice and Fanny, never one to suffer bores gladly, naughtily nicknamed him *Gâteau de Plomb*. She soon found, however, that if she placed him on a corner ottoman with gentle Dr. Nott he remained perfectly happy and did not interfere at all with the brilliant remarks that were tossed hither and thither by the rest of the company.

Thomas Anthony seldom appeared at these afternoon functions. He detested social flummery, as he called it, and was slightly scandalised that his wife should continue to entertain people outside her immediate family when her "condition" was becoming so obvious. But Fanny laughed at his remonstrances, told him he was getting into a rut, and declared nothing would induce her to give up her "At Homes" until it was time to send for doctor and midwife. Worried by his lack of briefs, racked by perpetual headaches, he longed for that day to come. When it did, bringing with it his longed-for son, he forgot all his woes and sat worshipfully by Fanny's bedside.

The boy must be named Thomas Adolphus (a delicate compliment to Uncle Meetkerke). He must start his classical studies at the earliest possible opportunity, go to Winchester and New College, become a Fellow and win a Vinerian Fellowship, read for the bar. In short, he must follow in his father's footsteps. Fanny ruffled the down on her son's head and wondered a little drearily where the money was going to come from; but she said nothing. In her year of marriage she had accumulated quite a store of wisdom.

(*iii*)

Thomas Anthony had been convinced that motherhood would have a steadying effect on his volatile wife, but he was speedily disillusioned. No sooner was she up and about again than she engaged a large, grim-faced woman called Farmer who was an Anabaptist, as nurse for Thomas Adolphus, pooh-poohed her husband's doubts as to the advisability of placing such an evangelical character in charge of their child, and resumed her social activities. Indeed, despite the fact that she started to have another baby within a very few months, these grew in intensity, for she was rapidly gaining the reputation of being a clever and delightful hostess at whose house interesting folk and good talk were always to be found. In 1811, exactly a year after Thomas Adolphus's arrival, her second son Henry was born, and although Cecilia, Anthony and Emily followed him in quick succession Fanny gathered around her an ever-increasing circle of friends.

She loved her children—of that there is no doubt whatsoever—but there was little maternal possessiveness about her love. She invented innumerable games to play with them and made first lessons an entrancing occupation by buying a lot of bone counters bearing alphabetical capital letters on one side and lower case letters on the other, then tossing them over the nursery floor and offering a prize to the child who brought her first the letter she asked for. She sang them quaint old songs, among them a particularly astonishing one about an "unfortunate Miss Bayly" who was seduced by a "Captain bold of Halifax, who dwelt in country quarters" and then, presumably overcome by her shame, committed suicide with the result that the parish priest had to be bribed with a one-pound note to bury her body in consecrated ground. She even, if legend is right, invented a delicious chorus about Farmer which ran:

> Old Farmer is an Anabap*tist*!
> When she has gone, she will not be missed!

The children, especially the two elder boys, adored this mother with the quick bright mind, the gay infectious laugh. Far from over-burdening them with rules and regulations she gave them only two—they must be obedient and they must not tell lies. She taught them to be independent and when they were still quite small allowed them to wander round the City from the Guildhall to the docks, to walk to Piccadilly in order to watch the coaches leave or arrive at the White Horse Cellar, and even, on one memorable occasion, to make an expedition to Saffron Hill market where supposedly all the pocket-handkerchiefs stolen by London pickpockets were displayed for sale.

Unfortunately the presence of Thomas Anthony acted on his family as effectively as the snuffers on the pewter tray in the dining-room acted on the tallow candles. In his way he was equally devoted, but a man of his irritable, melancholy temperament was the last person to enjoy a noisy nurseryful of babies, and they were the last people to enjoy him. When Thomas Adolphus was barely four years old his father was furious when he entered the bedroom to find the boy perched on a chair watching his mother dressing for dinner and overheard him say in a judicious voice as she put the finishing touches to her hair: "Now you have made yourself as fine as poso [possible] and you look worse than you did when you began!" He dismissed the child sharply, then turned to his wife. Had she no sense of the fitness of things to allow the boy such unfilial freedom of speech? Had she forgotten that the very next week he was to be taken to Julians for his first meeting with Uncle Meetkerke, who would assuredly pounce on the least fault in manners? Was she aware that owing to the laxity of their upbringing the children (apparently he included Cecilia who was a mere infant) were growing thoroughly unruly?

Fanny had become adept at soothing her husband and by the time the dinner-gong sounded he had relapsed into his usual melancholy, returning monosyllabic replies to her flow of chatter. Unfortunately she made some further allusion to Uncle Meetkerke which launched a second tirade, this time about the appalling backwardness of Thomas Adolphus. It was ridiculous that the child could barely read his own language. It was high time his classical education was begun. No doubt Uncle Meetkerke would wish to catechise him on his knowledge and his horror at the boy's ignorance might induce an apoplectic seizure. . . . It was at this point that Fanny, who had developed the habit of giving half her attention to her husband's discourses and the other half to household problems, murmured absent-mindedly that such a happening would lead to a solution of all their difficulties.

It was a monstrous, an unforgivable remark, regretted the instant it had been uttered. Thomas Anthony was outraged. That Fanny, his Fanny, the wife who had once remonstrated with him about his own behaviour towards Uncle Meetkerke, should harbour such terrible thoughts was incredible and although she spent the remainder of the evening protesting that her thoughts had been elsewhere, that she had not meant the words, that she was truly devoted to Uncle Meetkerke, it is doubtful if he ever forgot that unguarded phrase.

He went on loving her—there was the rub—but from that time forward he withdrew more and more into a world she could not penetrate, a sombre world filled with the shadows of his youthful hopes and dominated by the ghost of the Fanny Milton he imagined he had wooed at Heckfield Vicarage. In reality, of course, the Fanny Trollope of 1814 did not differ greatly from the Fanny Milton of 1808. She had matured naturally, but she was still the same creature of mercurial spirit, quick wit, and energetic ambition she had always been; and if the wit had sharpened, the ambition hardened, the fault lay in Thomas Anthony's stars rather than in her own. Probably it never occurred to the shy, lonely man that long before his visits to Heckfield he had built in his mind an image of the ideal woman and that when he was captivated by the vicar's daughter he automatically invested her with the attributes of that ideal; most assuredly he would have been deeply wounded had anyone told him how extraordinarily difficult he was to live with.

Outwardly he was still the dutiful if pompous husband: inwardly he was a resentful being who could not understand his unpopularity either with his colleagues or his family.

Concerning the dislike of his fellow-barristers he could do little; so, pathetically enough, he set about gaining the affection and admiration of his children.

His first few attempts met with singular lack of success. The role of jocular papa scarcely suited him and his suggestions of games to be played met with round-eyed stares from Thomas Adolphus and Henry, caterwaulings from Cecilia, and black looks from Farmer. Nothing daunted, Thomas Anthony bided his time and when Fanny was recovering from the birth of their third son, Anthony, he put into effect a pet plan she had been stalling ever since the scene about Uncle Meetkerke—the teaching of Latin to the two older boys, then aged five and four respectively. An ardent (one might almost say fanatical) Classical scholar himself, he simply could not conceive how any child could fail to be entranced by the learning of Latin grammar.

The Trollopes always breakfasted in the small back drawing-room—a habit started by the economical Fanny the first winter of her marriage in order to save lighting a fire in the dining-room—and the meal always started at 7.30 a.m. One day Thomas Anthony issued instructions that the boys were to parade in this room at seven o'clock punctually the following morning. They trailed in apprehensively (for who knew what fresh ordeal this ogre of a papa might have devised?) to be greeted with genial smiles and a rambling discourse of which they understood not one word. They were then presented with copies of the *Eton Latin Grammar,* told which passage to study, and dismissed with the stern injunction to return the next day at the same hour—with the passage committed to memory.

The result was, of course, disastrous. Henry could barely read one-syllable words in English, and his attempts at Latin were so hopeless that he was sent back to the nursery with the warning that torture was only deferred ringing in his ears, leaving poor Thomas Adolphus to bear the brunt of the attack. He was a bright child and anxious to please, so under the glare of his parent's bushy-browed eyes he stumbled through his task. (He told Henry afterwards "Papa was *worse* than poso.")

As he listened to the halting voice all the plans he had made at the time of his eldest son's birth flared anew in Thomas Anthony's brain. Here was malleable material and it was his duty to mould it. Gravely he outlined to the boy the course of studies he must follow in order to become that bright and shining being, a scholar of Winchester College. Thomas Adolphus nodded obediently. Even his infant mind realised that here was destiny, implacable, inescapable.

Every morning thereafter the hour of seven found him on his knees before the back drawing-room sofa with the *Eton Latin Grammar* propped on a cushion, trying desperately to get the relationship of relative and antecedent into his head before the footman came upstairs with the tea-urn and his father came downstairs for breakfast and the dreaded cross-examination on the previous day's work. The meal over, his father rose, set him a task for the day, drew out his heavy gold watch and admonished him to be at the Lincoln's Inn chambers by 4.30 p.m., when they would walk home together. This was no pleasurable experience, as Thomas Adolphus well knew, for the second step in his Classical education— playfully alluded to by his father as *Gradus and Parnassum*— was the turning of a line of English verse into Latin, and this was examined during the walk back to Keppel Street. Thomas Anthony walked very fast and with long strides; so his son trotted behind, struggling to keep pace yet save enough breath to answer this extraordinary form of *viva voce*. One of the lines given was "Muse and sound of wheel do not agree" which the child—with commendable agility—turned into *"Non bene conveniunt Musa rotaeque sonus."* This inspired one of Thomas Anthony's few flashes of wit, for he swung sharply round a corner into the quiet road by Featherstone Buildings saying, "Ha! That is exactly why I turned out of Holborn!"

(*iv*)

It may seem surprising that when Fanny came downstairs after Anthony's birth she did not nip this intensive cramming in the bud; yet there were many reasons for her lack of action. She had been brought up among scholars who revered the Classics and to her it was only natural that a boy should begin to learn Latin at a very early age. She believed also that the father should take as much part in the upbringing of children as the mother and was delighted by her husband's sudden parental zeal—surely it would lead to the metamorphosis in his character for which she had hoped so long? Again, there was something Spartan in her nature that approved a rigid discipline, almost a mortification, of mind and flesh. And there were lesser reasons too. With a rapidly growing family the keeping-up of appearances at 16 Keppel Street was no mean task and she would not, could not, give up her "At Homes," her occasional dinner-parties, her enlivening talks with some particular friend who was a figure in the great world of which, as yet, she knew so little. Thomas Anthony had ever been an exacting partner who demanded a great deal of her time and energy: now that his educational projects absorbed him she had far more opportunity both for domestic duties and social ploys.

One must remember she had suffered disappointments in her marriage which might have led a weaker character to despair. Thomas Anthony's moroseness, his failure to succeed at the bar, his unpopularity, his chronic headaches; these allied to nagging financial worries and the necessity for cheese-paring in every household department made her life one of continual struggle. Perhaps there was an element of selfishness in her decision not to interfere with her husband's new interest, but one cannot believe she realised at the time the fearful burden she was casting on Thomas Adolphus, the apple of her eye.

So the daily cramming went on and soon Henry was forced to join his brother both at morning devotions before the *Eton Latin Grammar* and on the dreaded afternoon walks from Lincoln's Inn, while Fanny's superhuman energy spent itself on cooking, dressmaking, mending and stimulating conversation. To her there was nothing incongruous in slaving for hours at menial jobs then sitting decorously in her drawing-room waiting for her guests to be announced by the liveried footman. Every family with decent social connections *had* to employ a manservant, and if asked the reason behind this edict she would have answered simply, "because the livery is *proper* to the Trollopes; it is not an *invented* one"; but at the same moment she was probably cogitating privately how on earth she was going to afford fruit for her dinner-parties now that the departure from London of General Guglielmo meant the cessation of his gifts of dried Neapolitan figs and Mandarin oranges.

For a time it really seemed as if Thomas Anthony's scholastic fervour was humanising him in a most satisfactory way. His headaches lessened in intensity, he talked more, he refrained from argument with dinner guests, and he was actually prevailed upon to undertake an occasional visit to the theatre, a treat vastly enjoyed by Fanny—although why she loved it so much is not clear since it was a real test of endurance. To begin with, since the hiring of a hackney carriage was out of the question, the journey had to be made on foot over dirty cobbled roadways, which spelt ruination to the hems of the sweeping dresses that were fashionable. Then, since pit seats were all the Trollopes could afford (with pardonable bravado Fanny always asserted that only from the pit could one achieve a thoroughly good view of the play) the theatre had to be reached by two o'clock in the afternoon although the performance did not start until six. Food had to be taken for consumption during the four-hour wait and as the crowd standing outside the door was so dense ladies fainted by the dozen and had to be removed by their male escorts. The homeward journey after the play was even more formidable than the outward one, for street-lighting was limited to a few flickering oil lamps, rogues and pickpockets abounded, and the night-watchmen whose duty it was to protect honest citizens were usually to be found asleep in their sentry-boxes, their huge rattles and stable-lanterns beside them. But despite the hardship theatre-going entailed Fanny adored it and for weeks afterwards would regale her children with an account of one of Mr. Macready's performances or a vivid imitation of Mrs. Siddons playing the part of Lady Macbeth.

All too soon, however, Thomas Anthony reverted to his former melancholy. While Fanny was staying at Heckfield with the three elder children he was again attacked by devastating headaches and, free of his wife's watchful eye, sought to cure them by swallowing enormous doses of calomel. If there be such a thing as calomel poisoning then he assuredly suffered from it, but in the light of present-day medical knowledge it seems certain that he had some deep-rooted internal disorder as well. In any event the family returned to find him in a violently irascible frame of mind and only too ready to vent his wrath on the two older boys. Ludicrously enough his first outburst was provoked not by neglect of their Latin studies but by their preoccupation with stage-coaches.

It was only to be expected that the boys should have been enchanted with the Reverend William's *Rotis volventibus*. Unfortunately, Thomas Adolphus worked the treadmill with such zest that the contraption ran away with him down a steep decline and he was rescued howling and covered with bruises. His kindly grandfather having said, "Never, Tom, put in motion forces which you are unable to control," comforted the child by showing him all the models in the coach-house and telling him wonderful tales of coach-development from earliest days down to the magnificent coaches then running all over the country. Naturally he came home chattering of "Telegraphs," "High-Flyers," "Magnets" and "Independents," of the marvellous celerity with which teams of horses were changed, of the route taken by the Falmouth mail, most famous coach of all. Naturally Henry followed his elder brother's example.

Thomas Anthony was beside himself with rage. To think, after all the efforts he had made to train their minds, that they should become obsessed with such foolish, puerile matters as the speed at which one could travel from London to Reading or the number of teams needed between Devonport and Falmouth. Fanny's mild assertion that at least these details taught them the geography of the native land went unheeded, and he ranted and roared at the children for a full two hours before retiring to bed with the worst headache he had ever known.

A few days later there was another storm caused by Thomas Adolphus' unpardonable forwardness. Dr. Nott was visiting the house and, as was usual, the children were summoned to he drawing-room so that he might question them as to their progress in lessons, their general behaviour, and their favourte games. He was devoted to children and they, for their part, had no least fear of the spare, kindly figure with the pale, delicate features, black gaiters and elaborate white neck-cloth. He was asking them solemnly, but with a twinkle in his eye, if they were always obedient to their nurse when Thomas Anthony appeared unnoticed in the doorway and was horrified to hear his eldest son answer just as solemnly hat they tried to be but that any backslidings must be attribated to the awful fact that Farmer was an Anabaptist. Dr. Nott began to explain that the nurse's particular faith was her own affair but Thomas Anthony swept the children from he room without more ado and followed them upstairs, where a terrific scene ensued.

It was then that Fanny realised what a deleterious effect Thomas Anthony produced on the nervous systems of Thomas Adolphus, Henry and Cecilia, and what a mistake he had made in not quashing the Latin lesson project at its tart. Now things had gone too far. He was determined to educate them as he thought they should be educated: they regarded him as a hated tyrant and no amount of argument on her part could convince them otherwise. All she could do was to try to protect the children from the father they feared and the father from the children who fretted him beyond endurance.

For all her courage, energy and intelligence Fanny was not he woman to deal with such a tricky situation. She possessed little sense of diplomacy, was impatient with people who did not grasp a point of view the moment it was put to them, and was apt to resort to subterfuge when she could not get her own way by straightforward means. Moreover the ambition which was so strong a part of her character convinced her that if she only did enough pushing and shoving of husband and family she could hoist them into the positions they ought to occupy. (Despite all the evidence to the contrary she still believed Thomas Anthony would rise to legal eminence.)

By dint of rising at an unconscionably early hour she managed to bustle through her household tasks at breakneck speed so that she might be able to linger at the breakfast table while her husband put the boys through their Latin catechism; but this move was not so successful as it should have been since she could not refrain from interrupting with remarks that verged on the sarcastic, and these wounded Thomas Anthony so sorely that he brooded over them until he developed the usual headache and staggered home from Lincoln's Inn to retire to bed where he lay, blinded by pain for two or three days.

Unconscious that she was the cause of these attacks Fanny nursed him briskly, whisked the calomel bottle out of sight when she had the opportunity, and told the boys to go off for a long walk. In the second decade of the nineteenth century it was a curious order to say the least, for no small children except street arabs roamed London streets unaccompanied by a grown-up; but Thomas Adolphus and Henry loved these expeditions and came home full of tales of magic things they had seen—the statues of Gog and Magog on Guildhall, a ship at East Indian dock being loaded for Bombay, the drovers and bullocks at Smithfield Market, the dead cat they had seen lying in a Whitefriars lane, the pickpockets of Saffron Hill, the coaches they had watched setting out from White Horse Cellar.

Fanny listened indulgently, unaware that Nemesis was about to overtake her. The Trollope boys were well known to the legal families living near Russell Square and many a lady twitched her lace curtains and tut-tutted as she saw them trotting past her window, and many a judge or barrister met them wandering round the Temple or staring up at the grim Fleet prison. Inevitably there was gossip; inevitably it reached the ears of Thomas Anthony, whose colleagues experienced a justifiable glee in telling the man who had so often picked quarrels with them in court, and out of it, that his sons had been seen *alone* in unsalubrious quarters of the city.

Thomas Anthony raged at Fanny for her gross neglect, her lack of maternal instinct, her odiously emancipated notions. She retaliated with sharp, stinging phrases which, alas, she forgot so soon as she had said them. Her husband did not forget. He nursed the words in his mind until they assumed a monstrous meaning they were certainly never intended to possess. Lying on his bed, a damp towel across his forehead, pain beating with hammer-like blows on his temples, he told himself over and over again that he was a failure, a creature shunned by his fellow-men, a husband and father shunned by his family.

He could not understand it. At Winchester, at New College, he had been liked by all. His scholarship was sound, he had always worked industriously, his knowledge of Chancery law had brought him many tributes. What then had gone wrong? He wanted so much to be loved by wife and children, venerated by legal acquaintances—yet people ran from him as though he were possessed by some evil spirit.

Poor Thomas Anthony! Perhaps because of his intense shyness, more likely because of the ailment which racked him, he was constitutionally incapable of showing his longing for affection, or of conciliating others, in order to win it. Consequently he developed a minor form of persecution mania which led him to lash back at anybody who had made even a mildly critical remark. By 1816 his friends at the bar could have been counted (literally) on the fingers of one hand: his enemies were legion. And this was entirely his own fault for he could not resist the saying of cruel and unjust things. Lord Eldon never forgave him for trumpeting abroad, "his mind is an instrument of admirable precision, but his soul is the soul of a pedlar." Jockey Bell, then considered the finest conveyancer in the country, cut him dead after hearing Trollope had said of him, "It is a dreadful thing to have to decipher an opinion of his. He is said to have three hand writings—one when he is sober, which he can read himself: one when he is drunk, which his clerk can read: and one next morning after being drunk, which no human being can read!" Even his whist-playing cronies refused politely when asked to join with him in a game, murmuring to each other "Many men will scold their partners occasionally. But Trollope invariably scolds us all round with the utmost impartiality; and that every deal!"

(v)

Peace came to England after Waterloo: about the same time peace departed from 16 Keppel Street. An aura of gloom wrapped the house around and even Fanny's determined brightness could not dispel it. When well enough Thomas Anthony stalked to his chambers, where no briefs awaited him and all he had to do was to count up the annual deficits on his practice, a depressing occupation since these had mounted steadily over the past six years. At home Fanny presided over the tea-table and offered Mr. Pidding's tarts to her guests while her thoughts revolved round the endless problems which beset her. By 1817 it was clear to her that the present state of affairs could not continue. However much she scrimped and scraped, the household expenses rose in alarming fashion. There were now five children whose education had to be allowed for (Emily, the youngest, had just made her appearance) and Thomas Adolphus and Henry ought to be having proper schooling instead of makeshift and irregular lessons at home. There was a definite worsening in Thomas Anthony's health which even her sturdy mind could no longer ignore, and he made no secret of the fact that if briefs did come his way he had neither the heart nor the physical strength to deal with them.

Something had to be done—and done quickly. If her husband remained in Keppel Street then the modest patrimony he had inherited from his father, the Reverend Anthony Trollope of Cottenham in Hertfordshire, would have to be broken into, in her opinion an unthinkable course for she knew too well how the money would dribble away in expensive London. Then an idea drifted into her fertile brain and the more she examined it the more it appealed. While capital should never be employed for running expenses, there were legitimate uses to which it could be put—and at this point the whole scheme sprang fully-armed, so to speak, from Fanny's mind. Thomas Anthony was sick, so the doctor had averred, because living in London did not suit him. Very well then, why not take a place in the country—fairly near London, of course—so that he could derive benefit from the air and yet drive up to his chambers each day? Why not have a farm to provide abundant fresh food for the family at infinitesimal cost?—then she remembered the very locality that would suit, Harrow-on-the-Hill. There, thanks to the generosity of one John Lyon, her three sons could attend the school as "town" or non-paying scholars and receive sound preparation for Winchester.

She lost no time in setting this remarkable proposition before Thomas Anthony, who naturally raised all manner of obstacles which were speedily demolished by his enthusiastic wife. The farm was bound to pay its way with people of their intelligence running it. He could buy a horse and gig for his daily journeys to and from London, and the good he would derive from so much fresh air would make him fit to conquer even that sour old Lord Eldon. The children would grow rosy and fat, the boys would triumph over their fellow scholars, she herself would superintend the farm workers. Finally, she knew that Lord Northwick, who owned much of the district, had a farm to rent.

She painted such a dazzling picture and pleaded her cause so ardently that Thomas Anthony capitulated. He was ill and tired, and whatever doubts his tortured brain held about Fanny he still loved her and had a profound belief in her business acumen. Negotiations were opened with Lord Northwick's men of business and a farm of some three or four hundred acres taken on a long lease. Since the existing farm-house was wholly inadequate another had to be built, so it was not until 1818 that the Trollopes left Keppel Street for Harrow-on-the-Hill. With her brood around her Fanny sat erect and shining-eyed in the fusty, rumbling hackney coach that carried them to their new home, her incurable optimism working like yeast within her. This time, she told herself, everything was going to be all right; this time there would be no heights she could not scale.

The Farmer's Wife

1818-1827

(i)

ONCE the vexatious business of moving was completed Thomas Anthony and all the Trollopes old enough to express an opinion declared themselves delighted with the Harrow house. Situated most pleasantly on the slope of a hill facing south, it had spacious, airy rooms, a nursery wing, and so many modern improvements that the London-bred servants felt themselves quite recompensed for their temerity in agreeing to follow their mistress to what they regarded as darkest Africa. The three elder children dashed round the surrounding fields in highest spirits while small fat Anthony toddled after them; Thomas Anthony walked round the farm with his bailiff, feeling very much the country gentleman; Farmer perambulated slowly up and down the gravel sweep by the front door with Emily in her arms.

Fanny beamed upon them all indulgently from the doorstep. She then turned back into the house, her glance darting hither and thither as she went from room to room. It was surprising how much more *light* there was here than in

Keppel Street—and how it showed up the shabbiness of curtains and furniture! Nobody would imagine that the drawing-room sofas and chairs had been new a brief nine years before. And surely that threadbare patch on the dining-room carpet had only just made its appearance? And was that ridiculously tiny hat-rack really the one which had looked so enormous in the Bloomsbury hall? Frowning slightly she sat down at her desk in the morning-room and began to make out a list headed "essential requirements." The actual building of the house had cost more than their most generous estimate had allowed for, but it would be a thousand pities if the place were to be spoilt for lack of a few finishing touches. Besides, in no time at all the farm would repay any extra money spent and also . . . Fanny shook her head and scribbled furiously. Not even to herself dared she admit the thought that had come unbidden into her mind *"after all, there is Uncle Meetkerke."*

Fanny had worked hard in Keppel Street: she worked ten times harder at Harrow. There were new curtains and chair-coverings to be made, new furniture to buy and arrange, a garden to plan, for she was determined that her lovely house should have its proper setting and not potato fields reaching to its windows. When the leasing of a farm had been first mooted she had, with commendable forethought, invested in a large volume on landscape gardening which she now put to practical use and every afternoon found her chivvying two stolid farm labourers who stared at her open-mouthed as she rattled off instructions about Italian gardens, Dutch gardens, and shrubs and flowers with incomprehensible names.

In the midst of all this activity Thomas Anthony announced lugubriously that the bailiff said the land was sour, the stock poor, the cottages and fencing in sad need of repair. Absorbed in her creation of the perfect garden and forgetful of the handsome profit the farm was to yield forthwith, Fanny gave a superb wave of the hand, saying that such matters must wait till she had time to attend to them and adding that since she had learnt all about gardening from one book it would be a simple affair to learn all about farming from another. Her husband sighed and drove off towards London in the gig he was beginning to hate, for in her exuberant praise of the benefits of fresh air Fanny had failed to take into account the vagaries of English weather and as often as not he was soaked to the skin before he reached Lincoln's Inn. To counteract the chills and shivers which beset him he bent his thoughts once more on the education of his children. Thomas Adolphus and Henry required more grounding in Latin before he could venture to ask Dr. Butler (afterwards Bishop of Peterborough), the Harrow Head Master, to accept them as pupils, while Cecilia and Anthony were old enough to start simple lessons.

So the early morning agonies with the *Eton Latin Grammar* began again and an extra horror was instituted, evening readings at which the father read extracts from some book in a voice devoid of all expression while the children sat still as mice. During the first winter at Harrow the book was *Sir Charles Grandison,* and ever afterwards the young Trollopes recoiled in loathing when they heard it mentioned. Not that Thomas Anthony was ever actively unkind to his family—long afterwards his eldest son wrote, "I never remember his caning, whipping, beating or striking any one of us"—but his whole personality was antipathetic. He had a habit of dangling one arm to and fro while reading or teaching and using this to tug the hair of any inattentive scholar, thus inducing an acute state of nervous apprehension in his victim; and he had a strain of asceticism in his nature which made him abhor the sight of anybody idling. Any child who had finished an allotted task ahead of time and run out to play was therefore severely reprimanded and marched back to the schoolroom to do an extra lesson, an imposition he or she considered grossly unfair.

Once more, alas, Fanny failed to intervene. The refurbishing of the house and the making of the garden absorbed her. Besides, the three older children had surely reached a stage when they were able to defend themselves, and her few leisure hours simply had to be devoted to the returning of calls; for if calomel was a drug to Thomas Anthony social activity was to Fanny as the daily dose to an opium eater and her one great regret at leaving Keppell Street had been the giving up of her "At Homes." Without exhilarating company she could not exist, and since many of her London friends flinched at the prospect of the costly, uncomfortable journey to Harrow she had perforce to form a new circle of local acquaintances.

First she wooed that formidable gathering of divines, the Harrow masters. Dr. Butler was certainly Head Master, but he had succeeded Dr. Drury and the school was still practically under the control of that gentleman's relatives. His brother Mark was second master, his son Harry fourth master, and Mark's son William fifth master. They were all in Holy Orders and each had a house into which they crammed as many boarders as they could find. Soon they and their wives, together with the three remaining masters (to whom Fanny paid small attention since they were not Drurys) were frequent guests at her afternoon parties, and Mark Drury had expressed his willingness to accept Thomas Adolphus as a "town," or non-paying day-boy the following term.

Fanny also made friends with a French envoy who had rented Lord Northwick's house and with a Mrs. Edwards, the wealthy and cultured widow of an antique bookseller.

These, with the Harrow School families and as many of her old friends as she could persuade to come to stay for a few days, were the nucleus around which she proceeded to build her new salon.

There was, however, one particularly large and buzzing fly in Fanny's social ointment. This was the Reverend Mr. Cunningham, vicar of Harrow, who arrived on the Trollope doorstep before they had been a week in the house and thereafter obstinately refused to be left out of any gathering. Rumour had it that he was the son of a London hatter who had purchased the living for him "under circumstances which were not altogether free from suspicion of simony." He himself bruited abroad the news that Lord Northwick had presented him with the living after hearing him preach, a statement greeted with derision by the Harrow masters who asserted that his lordship would not have attended church if the preacher had been St. Paul. Of handsome presence and with a suave, courtly manner, Mr. Cunningham was an evangelical, while the Drurys, though not High Churchmen in the present-day sense, belonged to what was known as the "high and dry" party. Moreover, Mr. Cunningham had published a little book under the title *The Velvet Cushion* which led the Drurys to nickname him "Velvet Cushion Cunningham," and had on one occasion rebuked Mark Drury's two pretty daughters from the pulpit, accusing them of giggling and saying he would resume the sermon when his congregation could listen to it with decency.

One can imagine what an unwanted guest Mr. Cunningham was in a Trollope drawing-room filled with Drurys! Harry, who was cousin to the two girls, never came within speaking distance of the vicar without growling "Brawler!," while the rest of the Harrow School faction lost no opportunity of raising controversial arguments. Fanny herself could not abide the man and knowing he was a great advocator of modern speech, her especial weapon against him was the employment of old-fashioned pronunciations when talking to him. Thus she deliberately said *obleege* for "oblige," *Room* for "Rome," *Jeames* for "James," *beefsteek* for "beefsteak," and used a short "a" (as in "man") in words such as "danger" and "stranger." But even this mode of attack failed to remove the odious Cunningham and he continued to call, on some pretext connected with the parish, every time he knew she was holding an "At Home."

(*ii*)

When the time came to go to school Thomas Adolphus sighed thankfully. At last he would be freed from the daily purgatory of lessons with Papa! To his consternation, however, he found he had jumped straight out of the frying-pan into the fire. Thanks to his parents' friendship with the Drurys and to the fact that he was too young to become a scholar at the school proper, it was arranged that he should go to Mark Drury's study each day. So powerful was that divine that he was allowed to teach his boarders in his own house at the bottom of the hill because his abnormal stoutness precluded him from climbing up to the school. As Thomas Adolphus was a non-paying pupil he sat behind the master's desk conning a task while the fortunate boarders received their lesson, and when the boarders filed out he was cross-examined alone for some ten minutes as the following class filed in.

It was too severe an ordeal for a small boy to bear. "Old Mark" was a kindly man at heart but professed a great belief in the rod and kept thundering at the child, "Your clock requires to be wound up every Monday morning!" which meant that a weekly flogging was necessary. This seldom took place because the maternal Mrs. Drury usually said that she had lost the key of the cupboard where the rods were stored. But the mere anticipation of it was enough to upset Thomas Adolphus. Again, "Old Mark" paid no heed to what the boys did outside his class and disapproved of prefects and fagging, with the result that his boarders took such advantage of their lowly brother that almost seventy years later he wrote: "How I hated it all! How very much more bitterly I hated it than I ever hated any subsequent school troubles! What a pariah I was among these denizens of Mark's and other pupil-rooms! For I was a 'town boy,' 'village boy' would have been a more correct designation. . . . I remember also, more vividly than I could wish, the bullying to which I was subjected at Harrow. There was much of a very brutal description."

So unhappy was Thomas Adolphus that he positively welcomed an illness which attacked him and his brother Henry. To Fanny's alarm this was diagnosed by the local doctor, who was really only an apothecary, as typhoid, and there was much agitation as to where the boys could have picked up the infection. Terrified lest the disease spread to the three younger children Fanny had a minute inspection of the plumbing in the new house carried out. This revealed no fault, but presently it transpired that the two had spent a happy hour one morning before breakfast watching some workmen clearing out an old drain at a near-by cottage. By a strange coincidence the doctor shared Thomas Anthony's passion for calomel, a medicine which had such an effect on Thomas Adolphus that he very nearly died. For days the distraught Fanny sat by his bed trying vainly to soothe him as he raved in his delirium about "Old Mark" coming to snatch him back to the classroom he feared and detested so much, and she was nearly at her wits' end when help appeared in the shape of a Dr. Butt, a relation of Mrs. Edwards who happened to be staying with her. "No more calomel, I think," he said gently to Fanny. "Let me have a glass of port wine instead." With a finger on the boy's pulse he administered the wine in a teaspoon and after a few days the patient began to mend, albeit slowly.

Fanny's gratitude was intense, and to the end of her long life she sang the praises of the man who had saved the life of her beloved eldest son; yet despite the acute anxiety she had suffered, including the piteous revelations the child had made while delirious, she not only packed him back to "Old Mark" before he was fully convalescent but sent Henry with him!

One may well wonder why such a genuinely devoted mother should have deliberately sent her children to a place where they were so utterly wretched; but Fanny was a strangely contradictory character. On the surface she was a creature of impulse given to strange enthusiasms and possessing the enviable faculty of throwing off sorrows and troubles without the slightest difficulty; yet underneath the gaiety, the wit, the restless dartings after new friends and interests lay a grimly ambitious mind that did not hesitate to sacrifice anybody or anything in order to gain a certain end. The years in Keppel Street had not altered her much, but the move to Harrow had wrought a basic change in her. It had destroyed the illusion around which she had built the whole of her married life, the illusion that Thomas Anthony would one day meet with success. Within a very few months of settling into the new house he had found the daily drive to and from London an intolerable physical strain and soon his visits to Lincoln's Inn fell first to two, then to one a week. Not that this mattered, for no briefs graced his desk when he reached it. His efforts to manage the farm were singularly unsuccessful and by the time that Thomas Adolphus and Henry had recovered from their illness he was a man broken in heart and body, a man moreover with a temper so irascible that it was well-nigh impossible to live with him.

Even Fanny could no longer cherish dreams of the Woolsack. Characteristically she immediately threw aside all her deep-laid plans for her husband's advancement and began to form others. If Thomas Anthony had proved himself incapable of success there was all the more reason why she and the children must concentrate upon winning it. There was no time to be lost—not a moment—for it was quite astounding what a large slice of Thomas Anthony's patrimony had vanished in their first two years at Harrow.

So the mother who had sat agonised by her eldest son's bedside and who had existed in a state of sheer terror for months lest something dreadful should happen to her family after the French envoy's messenger had been murdered on the road from London, paid absolutely no attention to the two elder boys' unhappy faces and still weakly bodies. Instead she dinned it into them daily that it was their bounden duty to amass all the learning they possibly could, dismissed their feeble protests with brusqueness, and sent to London for a ponderous tome on farming.

She had always been energetic: now there was something relentless about her passionate efforts to lift her husband, her children and herself out of the Harrow doldrums into which, to be honest, her own impulsiveness had led them. By seven o'clock each morning she was bustling round the farm, clad in her oldest clothes, arguing about this, complaining about that, discoursing on crops or cattle or poultry, scolding the bailiff for his lazy habits or the labourers for their slowness. From being a careful housekeeper she became a positively parsimonious one who derived enjoyment from effecting the smallest economy. Her wretched sons tramped unwillingly to school garbed in patched, cut-down suits of their father's and clod-hopper boots which drew many ribald jests from their more fortunate fellows.

(*iii*)

Fanny's whirlwind methods had such excellent results for the farm—or so she thought at the time—that she decided on a well-earned rest and announced to her startled husband that he, Thomas Adolphus and herself would spend the long summer vacation "touring" the counties of Sussex, Hampshire, Wiltshire, Somerset and Devon. The cost, she added briskly, would be infinitesimal since the gig would hold the three of them and George, the footman, could be turned into a groom and ride behind with a second horse and a pair of traces to hook on as tandem when bad hills were encountered. Thomas Anthony's reaction was one of dismay—he detested being pulled out of his melancholy solitude—but his wife was adamant. Telling him the trip would be good for his health she made all the arrangements. She wrote to her cousins, the Misses Fanny and Mary Bent of Exeter, announcing that they would arrive there on a certain date.

Thomas Adolphus, of course, was excited at the prospect. Why, he would see that wonderful coach the "Quicksilver," watch the teams being changed, pass through all the towns and villages of which he had heard so much from Grandfather Milton! On the morning of departure he was up before daylight, fuming and fretting lest they leave the start too late to reach Dorking that night, and when at last he was seated on a little box placed between his parents' knees he assured his mother that he was "as happy as a prince." So he was, poor child, for some ten miles. Then his father pulled a Delphin Virgil from his pocket, said sombrely that travel was not at all incompatible with study and intimated that he was ready to hear Thomas Adolphus construe.

For once Fanny was on the side of the angels and told him sharply that he must not spoil the child's holiday; but Thomas Anthony, still nursing his wrath at being dragged on this ridiculous expedition, retorted as sharply that election to Winchester lay less than twelve months ahead. So for the rest of the day Thomas Adolphus sat huddled on his little box aching to watch the miraculous scenes unfolding as they drove, yet forced to concentrate on Virgil. That evening, however, Fanny's tongue was so barbed with sarcasm that with an ill grace her husband agreed to reserve further lessons for the days when the little party were not actually in motion.

Since the strictest economy was necessary they lunched frugally off bread and cheese and stayed overnight at small, cheap inns. In Gloucester they nearly lost Thomas Adolphus altogether, because they took him to the cathedral a quarter of an hour before Sunday morning service in order to see the great bell being rung. In those days there was one huge rope which divided into seven pieces—one for each of the bell-ringers—about twelve feet from the pavement in the body of the church. On this particular morning one ringer had failed to appear. The sight of his dangling rope proved too much for the boy and he rushed forward and seized it in an effort to help. Unfortunately at that very moment the six stalwart men were at the end of their pull. They had released their ropes with the result that Thomas Adolphus was swung up to the ceiling at terrific speed. Immediately all was pandemonium. Fanny screamed, the men yelled to the child to hold on tight, Thomas Anthony dashed hither and thither beseeching everyone in sight to save his son. Luckily the roof was so high that the boy did not reach it before the swing of the bell returned him safely to the ground, so exhilarated that it was only with difficulty that he was restrained from trying the experiment again.

Unbeknown to his father Thomas Adolphus was secretly reading the *Mysteries of Udolpho,* given to him by Fanny as an antidote to Virgil, and his mind was so full of the marvellous adventures enjoyed by Mrs. Radcliffe's heroes that his dearest ambition was to experience dangers himself. Gloucester Cathedral provided him with one experience and a second experience occurred when driving down a steep hill at Lynton. Only a low wall of loose stones formed a barrier between the road and a precipice. The horse, which had taken fright at something, suddenly dashed at the wall and actually put its fore-feet over it. With most unusual presence of mind Thomas Anthony leapt from the gig, caught the animal by the bridle, and dragged it back on to the road.

Apart from these incidents their long journey was both pleasant and exciting, and in the soothing atmosphere of the Bents' Exeter home the three Trollopes felt more gentle towards each other than they had done for quite a time. Thomas Adolphus ran wild, gorged himself on strawberries and cream, made friends with Lucy Bowring (daughter of Dr. Bowring as he was then), and a little girl called Rachel Hutchinson, who was deeply evangelical and attempted to save his soul by presenting him with a volume of Low Church literature. Thomas Anthony had long talks with the local clergy, some of whom he had known in youth, and cheered up mentally and physically in consequence. As for Fanny, she embarked on a series of delicious excursions to Marypole Head, Haldon Down, Upton Pines and the valley of the Exe, while the scintillating conversation of the many visitors to her cousins' house filled her with delight.

Also, and perhaps most important, the companionship of her elderly cousin Fanny acted like balm on a mind which, though resilient, had been sorely scarred by the bitter disappointments of the past several years. Of Miss Mary Bent, a younger half-sister, we know little, but Miss Fanny was a remarkable character. Very plain-looking, badly off, clothed always in rough home-spun garments of Quakerish appearance, she was a fervent Conservative and churchwoman and possessed such a strong personality that, as Sir John Bowring said later, she was as much an Exeter landmark as the cathedral towers. People young and old flocked to her house, either to seek her wise advice or to listen entranced to her shrewd and humorous talk. Like others of her generation she preferred to speak in the dialect of her native county and one of her most popular accomplishments was the recitation of "Peter Pindar's" description of the King's visit to Exeter ... *"Nate, nate! Clane, clane!* Do ye mop it, mop it, Mister *Dane?"* and *Dane* Buller's answer which entranced Thomas Adolphus, "In all our Ex'ter shops we do not meet with such long mops. Our mops don't reach so high!"

Generous, warm-hearted Fanny Bent undoubtedly helped the mercurial Fanny Trollope a great deal, and on the long drive homeward to Harrow she treated both husband and son with unaccustomed gentleness.

(*iv*)

This softened mood did not endure. It blew away on the chill September wind which greeted the trio's arrival, for on the very doorstep Fanny walked into a host of troubles. Emily had a chest cold which refused to be shaken off. Anthony had tumbled into a disused well and had injured a foot. Farmer and the cook had had a quarrel. The household bills had spiralled in the most alarming manner. And outdoors the situation was worse, much worse. Thunderstorms had flattened the grain before it could be harvested, two cows had sickened and died of a mysterious complaint, cottages and fences needed repair, the bailiff wished to leave.

Before removing her bonnet and mantle Fanny examined Anthony and Emily, scolded Farmer and the cook, made a lightning inspection of the farm and told the bailiff the sooner he went the better she would be pleased. Then she marched upstairs, put on her oldest clothes, and descended to give battle. The indomitable Mrs. Trollope had returned with a vengeance!

From that moment Fanny's real struggles with the Harrow farm began. In her girlhood days at Heckfield she had kept chickens, but this ploy could scarcely be regarded as sufficient training for the running of a three or four hundred acre farm, and while it had been fairly simple to plan a pleasant garden with the aid of a book and a certain amount of money she found that the building up of a successful farm with the aid of a book and *without* money was a far more formidable problem. She was much too impatient to make a good farmer. She refused to make allowances for floods or drought, for severe winters or cold summers and was highly indignant with the elements when they did not behave according to her needs. Her quicksilver energy and agility of mind entirely dazed the slow-witted labourers, who grew both to fear and dislike her and therefore scamped their tasks whenever opportunity offered. Finally, she suffered from a sort of *folie de grandeur* about the farm, insisting that everything on it, from stock and seed to implements, should be of the very latest and best variety.

From the beginning, of course, the whole affair had been a hopeless proposition, but Fanny was not the one to admit defeat and she moiled and toiled like a woman possessed while Thomas Anthony brooded in his library about an enormous *Encyclopaedia Ecclesiastica* he had long planned to write. Meanwhile, Thomas Adolphus was elected a scholar of Winchester, Anthony reluctantly followed Henry to "Old Mark's," Cecilia and Emily developed ominous coughs and the house, with the exception of the drawing-room, stayed shabby and neglected.

It was small wonder that she became known to the genteel inhabitants of Harrow as "that eccentric Mrs. Trollope." In her day ladies of quality did not tramp around their own land performing ploughmen's tasks; much less did they forsake this revolting occupation one afternoon each week in order to entertain the cream of the neighborhood. Imagine a hostess who smelt of the stable, or worse still, the pig-sty! But Fanny had no intention either of pandering to gentility or forsaking her cherished "At Homes" and it says a great deal for her personality that people still angled for invitations to these parties.

Yet even in her own drawing-room Fanny's tongue got her into hot water on more than one occasion and, as usual, the Reverend Mr. Cunningham was a useful butt for her caustic wit. Once, when he was not present and she had been inveighing against him, a very pretty young girl rushed to his defence and told how he had swept away all her doubts about dogma and creed. Fanny glanced up and fixed her with a bright, bird-like gaze. "Did he kiss you, Carrie?"

"Yes—yes, Mrs. Trollope," stammered Carrie. "He *did* give me the kiss of peace. I am sure there was no harm in that!"

"None at all, Carrie," retorted Fanny, "for I am sure you meant none. *Honi soit qui mal y pense.* But remember,

Carrie, that the kiss of peace is apt to change its quality if repeated!"

Needless to say this remark was repeated, with embellishments, and did not endear Mrs. Trollope to the vicar or his adherents; but a greater storm was to follow when the body of Allegra, Byron's natural daughter by Claire Clairmont, was sent home from Italy for burial in Harrow Church. Amid much agitation the vicar presided over a large meeting in the vestry and here, for once, the High and Low Church partisans were in agreement that no headstone with the poor little child's name on it should mark the place where her remains rested, their extraordinary reason being that such a memorial might tend to injure the morals of the Harrow schoolboys! Despite this decision Cunningham, a toady to his backbone, wrote a letter to Lord Byron saying that on reading *Cain,* then scandalising the public, he had "felt a profound admiration for the genius of the author." He then went to Harry Drury, Byron's old tutor and friend, and asked him to forward this communication. Drury read the letter and raised his eyebrows. "Did you indeed *admire Cain?* I think it the most blasphemous publication that ever came from the pen"—and he point-blank refused to send on the document.

The vestry meeting and its consequences were received by Fanny with puckish glee and she forthwith wrote a long satirical poem of some five hundred verses describing all the characters in the affair in the most pointed terms. Harry Drury, though Fanny had not spared him, was so tickled with her effort that he presented her with a quarto page on which Byron had written the poem, "Weep, daughters of a royal line," beginning with a stanza that had been suppressed by the publishers. Round the edges of the page was a signed inscription stating the verses "were copied for my friend, the Rev. Harry Drury." Fanny kept this as one of her dearest possessions, and impulsively showed both it and her own poem to various friends. The results were a smouldering feud between the vicar and herself (she wrote of it many years later in *The Vicar of Wrexhill*); a violent conflict between the High and Low Churchmen of the district; and a deal of scandal among those who had already dubbed her "eccentric."

Through the early eighteen-twenties the financial situation of the Trollopes steadily worsened. No matter how heroically Fanny worked, the farm simply would not pay. Farmer was dismissed and an "indigent gentlewoman" installed to look after Cecilia and Emily. George the footman went and the gig and horses were sold. Henry and Anthony slouched through the lanes to school looking more than ever like farmworkers' children. Thomas Anthony began work on his encylopaedia, only emerging to torture his children with the dreaded cross-examinations on their lessons. Thomas Adolphus, happy and moderately successful at Winchester, was the only bright spot in his mother's troubled world. Fanny was just arranging to take him to Julians where Uncle Meetkerke would doubtless be overwhelmed by the boy's charm of manner and brilliance of mind, when Aunt Meetkerke died.

Fanny had thought often enough of the death of *Uncle* Meetkerke; but it had somehow never occurred to her that his elderly wife would suddenly take off her green riding-habit for the last time and die within a day or two. The news led to a long argument between herself and Thomas Anthony. She contended that, as the heir, he must journey post-haste to Julians to comfort the bereaved old gentleman: he protested that his attendance at the funeral was surely all that was required. As usual, Fanny got her way, which was unfortunate because her husband arrived in Hertfordshire with a blinding headache that sadly affected his temper and he spent the evening in acrimonious political debate with his uncle and his lawyer cousin, John Young. Whether this had anything to do with subsequent events we do not know, though Fanny always swore it had *everything* to do with them, but after six months' silence Uncle Meetkerke wrote a sprightly letter announcing his marriage to a young and buxom lady. Within a year this new Mrs. Meetkerke gave birth to a son, the first of six children!

Here indeed was the death-knell to all the Trollopes' hopes. From his youth up Thomas Anthony had been his uncle's acknowledged heir, and there had therefore been some justification for his renting of the farm and his building of the Harrow house. Now he was faced with disaster, and to do him justice he accepted the blow with dignity, uttering no word of abuse or regret. Not so Fanny, who flew into a furious rage which affected every member of the household. One moment she condemned Uncle Meetkerke for his abominable perfidy, the next moment she accused Thomas Anthony of deliberately antagonising the old man. Then she demanded to know what was going to happen to her five starving children. For a week the storm shook the walls of the library, but it died as swiftly as it had been born, for Fanny had just thought of a new plan.

On one of her rare visits to London she had met General Lafayette and his two wards, the Misses Camilla and Frances Wright, and made such friends with them that Frances at least had stayed several times at Harrow while the General had repeatedly asked the Trollopes to pay a visit to La Grange, his estate in France. Miss Frances Wright, a statu-esque, almost masculine beauty who favoured the wearing of Turkish trousers and had written a successful small book entitled *A Few Days in Athens,* had poured into Fanny's ears details of an astonishing scheme to which she wished to devote her considerable fortune. Under the influence of her great friend, Robert Dale Owen, she had conceived a passion to emancipate the Negro slaves of the Mississippi Valley, and proposed to buy an estate there on which she would found a free and ideal community.

Fanny remembered that plan now, and the more she thought over it the more she was convinced that the solution of all her troubles was at hand. She was out of love with her farming struggles, Henry and Emily were beginning to show signs of the distressing disease which was to cut both their lives lamentably short (but the word "tuberculosis" was never mentioned in the Trollope household), Thomas Anthony was wedded to his singularly unprofitable encyclopaedia, Thomas Adolphus was shortly going up to New College, Anthony was at Harrow, Cecilia was rapidly growing up. It was the very time to make a move, decided Fanny briskly, and where better could they move to than that rich and fabulous land of America about which people were beginning to talk so much? Without more ado she wrote to General Lafayette asking if she, Thomas Anthony and Henry might visit him in France.

The General was delighted. Fanny started packing and answered her husband's melancholy grumbles by telling him bluntly that the remarriage of Uncle Meetkerke was entirely his fault, that if he had any affection for his children he would welcome the idea of joining Miss Wright's scheme, and that with the small remaining capital they had left they could, under her capable management, make their fortunes in the new world.

The visit to La Grange was, in Fanny's eyes at least, an unqualified success. Despite the General's objections Frances

Wright had already bought an estate called Nashoba near Memphis in Tennessee and had visited it. She was going to rechristen it New Harmony and, with the aid of several enthusiastic helpers, make it into a paradise on earth. Within a very short time Fanny had enrolled herself, Henry, Cecilia and Emily as members of this emancipatory band and returned home to make all the necessary arrangements before starting on her new venture.

Once again the ruthless streak in her nature came to the fore. Thomas Anthony may have been an unsuccessful barrister but he was an even less successful farmer and Fanny knew this perfectly well. Yet when she found there was no way of getting out of their long lease from Lord Northwick she promptly took a smaller farm at Harrow Weald and told him brutally that he could run both places while she prepared a future home for the family in Nashoba. She then let the original Harrow house to—of all people!—her ancient enemy Mr. Cunningham, and moved Thomas Anthony and the furniture to the rather tumble-down house on the Harrow Weald farm.

The thought of leaving the twelve-year-old Anthony to the care of his irascible, intolerant father troubled her not at all. He was the sturdiest of her flock and, one regrets to record, the child she loved least. Perhaps even then she recognised the latent power within him and instinctively resented it. Ignoring alike the child's tears and Thomas Anthony's moans she scuttled through the days in a flurry of packing, repacking, booking of passages and issuing of last-minute instructions until the arrival of the majestic but fanatical Frances Wright. On November 4th 1827 she sailed with that lady, Henry and her two daughters, from London in the sailing-ship *Edward*.

One doubts if she bade the remaining members of her family more than a cursory farewell: one is sure they faded from her thoughts before the ship gained the English Channel. As she gazed from the deck at the scudding seas there was only one thought in Fanny's mind—she was going to the Promised Land.

The Doubtful Traveller

1827-1828

(i)

IT TOOK the *Edward* a full seven weeks to battle her way across the Atlantic, but Fanny, filled with the ardour of the true crusader, enjoyed every moment of the voyage. For the first time in ten years she was free of the twin anxieties of the Harrow farm and Thomas Anthony's health. She was an excellent sailor and the plungings and tossings of the ship induced in her a sense of exaltation. Hour after hour she sat in the ladies' saloon with Miss Frances Wright, listening eagerly as that ideal companion explained in booming tones how she felt it her duty to bury herself for life "in the deepest forests of the western world, that her fortune, her time, and her talents might be exclusively devoted to aid the cause of the suffering Africans." Nature, so Miss Wright declared oracularly, had made no difference between black people and white except in the pigmentation of their skins. What right then had humanity to draw any dividing line between African and Caucasian? It was her mission to establish a half-black, half-white colony and to educate all the children together and equally, thus proving beyond doubt that the brain of the Negro was as good in every way as the brain of his white classmate. Once this fact was dinned into thick American and European heads, slavery would be abolished and the Africans would take their proper place in the civilised world.

Fanny, who had never even seen a Negro at close quarters, was thrilled by this exposition of the theories of Robert Dale Owen. Life at Nashoba, where Miss Wright's sister was already established, was going to be wonderful indeed. And what an opportunity for dear delicate Henry, who was to become a teacher in the black-and-white school! As she slithered round the deck in the teeth of a northeast gale Fanny's mind held a vision of her second son, famous and adored by all, lecturing on his Nashoba achievements to vast gatherings in London, Paris, Berlin, Rome. . . .

It was a trifle disconcerting, of course, to find on her infrequent and perilous descents to the family cabin that neither dear Henry nor his sisters were in a fit state to share her enthusiasm. For to the Trollope children the voyage so enjoyed by their mother was as a foretaste of hell. Henry and Cecilia proved deplorable sailors while small Emily was utterly terrified by everything about her strange new way of life. The three lay huddled in their bunks, too wretched to swallow the rough but wholesome food brought them by a kindly steward, too apathetic to do more than close their eyes when their parent whirled into the cabin accompanied by a gust of icy, salty air.

For the first few days the preoccupied Fanny comforted herself with the thought that *all* children suffered seasickness. She looked after them in her usual brisk fashion, saw that they had plenty of fresh water to sip, plumped up their pillows, gave them grey powders and wrapped their heads in

newspapers in an effort to avoid the distressing mess result-
ing from their illness. But when the *Edward* was over a week
out of London and there was still no improvement in their
condition she became more than a little annoyed. It was
absurd, she lectured the three mute figures, to give way to
either mental or physical weakness and it was high time they
roused themselves, put on warm clothes and took a turn on
the deck. Good fresh air was what they needed. It would
blow the cobwebs away in no time and give them gargantuan
appetites for the dinner of lentil soup and salt pork she
knew was being prepared.

The mere mention of food caused Henry and Cecilia to
turn their faces to the wall and Emily to burst into tears.
Fanny tut-tutted in vexation and tried another tack. Surely
they realised the selfishness of their behaviour? They really
must make some effort to help poor Mama, who had left
Papa, Thomas Adolphus, Anthony, her home, her friends,
everything, in order to start a fresh life for them all in a new
country. Henry especially (here Fanny could not resist a
touch of drama) should be grateful for the marvellous career
Mama had planned for him at Miss Frances Wright's school.
Why, just think, in a few years' time he would be hailed as
the liberator of a downtrodden race now forced to live in
degradation, he would . . . .

But the doctrines of Mr. Owen held no appeal for the
young Trollopes. Henry pulled the blankets over his ears,
Cecilia was violently sick, Emily howled louder than before.
The exasperated Fanny flounced out of the cabin and as she
clung spiderwise to the ladder-rail she pondered the gross
ingratitude of the young. The idea that she was deliberately
sacrificing her children, particularly Henry, on the altar of
her own ambition did not cross her mind; she was concerned
only with their failure to recognise the glory of the brave new

world to which she was taking them. Feeling a sudden need for sustenance for both mind and body she made her way to the dining-saloon, there to learn to her chagrin that even the invincible Miss Wright had succumbed to seasickness.

Fortunately that lady's protégé, a youthful Frenchman named Auguste Hervieu, was one of the few passengers at table and his stimulating conversation soon removed Fanny's temporary fit of melancholy. Hervieu had studied art in Paris, where he had won much praise from his masters, but he had become so infected with enthusiasm for Miss Wright's schemes that he had begged to be allowed to accompany her to Nashoba and to instruct the children in the rudiments of drawing. But this admirable work, so he assured Fanny with a wealth of gesture, was only the prelude. From what he had heard and read America offered magnificent opportunities to the painter of historical scenes—a subject he was more interested in than any other—and on his first vacation he proposed to journey to Cincinnati, the western metropolis situated on *La Belle Rivière,* as he understood the Ohio river was called, and paint a noble picture of General Lafayette's memorable landing at that city. Naturally the Cincinnati burghers would immediately purchase the canvas for a large sum; equally naturally every other city in America would clamour for similar paintings.

Fanny was entirely captivated by M. Hervieu's plans (how she wished dear Henry would display the same sturdy determination to succeed!) and for the rest of the voyage she and the Frenchman were boon companions. Together they explored the *Edward* from bow to stern until they knew the name of every sail and the use of every pulley; together they exclaimed at the beauty of ocean dawn or sunset; together they made up little jokes about minor hardships—the saltness of the beef, the hardness of the biscuits, the mildew that ruined half the pages in the books they had brought, the smallness of the quarter-deck round which they perambulated like asses in a mill. By the time the *Edward* glided into the smooth blue waters of the Gulf of Mexico they were firm friends.

There was tremendous excitement when the sailors at last shouted "Land Ahoy!" The passengers, wearied of the long voyage, scurried on deck to watch the pilot come aboard. But where, demanded the dismayed Fanny as she peered over the rail at a swirl of muddy yellow water, was the land? Silently one of the crew pointed to long stretches of mud on which stood large numbers of pelicans. They looked sullen, unfriendly birds, and for a wild moment she thought that the whole desolate scene would have inspired Dante to describe another *bolgia*. Then she gave herself a little shake, for such dark imaginings would never do. Clambering down to the cabin she flung open the door: "'Henry, Cecilia, Emily! Come quickly, quickly, we are at the mouth of the Mississippi River!"

If she had said they were at the gates of heaven she could not have received a more astonishing response. The children, who had long been sure they were condemned for evermore to a sick, miserable existence in this ghastly ship, leapt from their bunks, grabbed at their outer garments, and followed their mother up the ladder. Leaning over the rail they bombarded one of the ship's officers with eager questions. Henry was intrigued by sight of a mast sticking out of the water, a grim reminder of a vessel wrecked in crossing the bar; Cecilia was charmed by the pelicans; Emily was fascinated by the enormous bulrushes growing out of the mud banks and insisted they hid a second infant Moses; all three were thrilled to see crocodiles lying in the slime and to watch the huge trees, uprooted by some recent hurricane, floating swiftly downstream.

Strangely enough, Fanny was the only member of the family who drew no pleasure from this first view of America. To her there was something indescribably sinister about the great muddy river, the swamps on either side of it, and the huddle of derelict huts called the Balize, where the families of pilots and fishermen fought a ceaseless battle against poverty and pestilence. Resolutely she pushed foreboding to one side and tried to listen intelligently to the captain's lecture about the levées. These high embankments were made to protect the sugar-growing lands from encroachment by the Mississippi. They stretched from the Balize to a hundred miles beyond New Orleans, a total distance of some two hundred and twenty miles, and while doubtless they were very necessary they gave the river traveller the sensation of being enclosed between two towering, colourless walls.

Navigation was difficult and the two days it took the *Edward* to reach New Orleans seemed to Fanny longer than any week of their Atlantic voyage. Always the landscape looked the same—the swamps, the crocodiles, the occasional cluster of huts, the monstrous bulrushes, the dun bluff of the levée shutting out any view. "There is not one inch," said M. Hervieu in a melancholy voice, "of what painters call a second distance." Fanny sighed. What if she had done the wrong thing? What if the whole of America contained no "second distance"?

Perhaps Miss Wright sensed her friend's apprehension. Anyway, the evening before they were due to arrive at New Orleans she chose to deliver a most eloquent and stirring speech about the immense possibilities latent in the new world. These could only be translated into reality, she averred, by the determined efforts of Europeans courageous enough to wage war against the corruption, ignorance and superstition then prevalent among those Americans who were opening up and cultivating the western and southern regions of their country. Listening to her deep, rich voice, and looking at her dark, flashing eyes, Fanny's feeling of foreboding dwindled and died. Once more adventure beckoned and by the time bedtime came she had regained all the crusading spirit which had animated her during her visit to La Grange. Marching down to the cabin she retailed Miss Wright's words to her family, and as she climbed into her bunk she murmured, as though it were an incantation:

"Tomorrow to fresh woods, and pastures new."

(ii)

The Trollopes landed at New Orleans on December 27th, and they had a few days in which to explore the city because Miss Frances Wright had much business to transact before proceeding upriver to Memphis. Fanny no longer had cause to complain of her children's lethargy. Like prisoners released from long bondage they exclaimed in wonderment at the miracles which met their eyes—the laughing black people thronging the streets, the elegant quadroons who seemed to glide rather than walk, the wild, fine-featured Indians in their native dress, the haunting songs of the Negro stevedores and boatmen that rose above the clamour of the waterfront, the colourful market with its stalls piled high with melons, oranges, red peppers and other exotic fruits and vegetables never seen in England, the sudden downpours of tropic rain, the hot sun which shone in bursts of splendour from a deep blue sky. "Mama, come and look!" was their constant cry; but while Fanny nodded automatically and added her quota of praise she could not share their glowing view of everybody and everything in New Orleans.

She refused to admit it even to herself, but she was disappointed with both people and city because they were so different from her dreams of them. Despite all the vicissitudes she had known in the eighteen years of her marriage she had lived in a narrow world governed by certain strict rules of behaviour. Now she found herself in a community entirely heedless of these rules and she did not, could not, approve such laxness. From the moment she stepped ashore from the *Edward* she had been aware of a certain sprawling quality about New Orleans. Everything seemed to sprawl—the buildings, the vegetation, the great turbid river, the slow southern speech of the inhabitants. "New Orleans," she wrote acidly in her diary, "presents very little that can gratify the eye of taste."

She was disturbed too by "the most violent, and the most inveterate prejudice" of the rich Louisiana creoles against the charming quadroons. Her alert mind was quick to discern the fact that practically all these gentle people, although rigidly excluded from any creole gathering, were the result of happy but illict unions between white men and women with some strain of Negro blood. Still filled with crusading fervour Fanny considered that the social ban against the quadroons was grossly unfair. She feared the effect even a brief stay in this flamboyant city of racial hatreds might have on the impressionable Henry, Cecilia and Emily. She announced therefore that they would spend their days exploring the huge forest which lay near the town.

It cannot be said that these expeditions were entirely successful. The walk to the forest was long and hot, and undertaken reluctantly by the children who would far rather have pottered about the market or waterfront. In the forest itself the atmosphere was unbearably humid, the mosquitoes attacked in droves, the trees were twisted, stunted growths festooned with a feathery parasitical creeper known as "Spanish Moss." Cecilia and Emily derived a mild pleasure from swinging on the tough, pendant ropes of wild vines, but this soon palled owing to the attention of a variety of insects. Not all their mother's eulogies on the beauty of the palmettos and pawpaw shrubs which formed the luxuriant undergrowth could make them forget the prickly heat, the itching bites.

One afternoon as they trailed homewards Fanny's eye was attracted by a bright flowery hedge surrounding a well-stocked garden. Never backward, she marched her family through the gateway that they might see the oranges ripening in the sun, the rows of fat green peas, the sturdy crop of red peppers—all ready for eating in the end of December! The only person in sight was a young Negress sweeping the steps in front of the house. Realising that she was a slave, Fanny exhorted the children to be most gentle with her and immediately entered into conversation about the garden. To her astonishment the girl answered gaily, without the least sign of fear, laughed at her interest in red peppers and gave Emily several pods. Fanny, whose ideas on slavery were gleaned from Miss Wright's diatribes, tried to return the gift on the grounds that the girl's owners might punish her severely, but the Negress merely smiled and waved them a happy goodbye from the gate. Hitherto Fanny's doubts about America had been confined to New Orleans and the Mississippi: now, as she plodded on towards the city, she knew her first qualm about Nashoba. Something which happened the next day increased her unease.

New Orleans' most fashionable milliner was a young English woman of great intellectual attainments who discussed metaphysics with her friends as easily as she talked of the latest modes with her French-speaking customers. Delighted by such versatility Fanny asked if she might be introduced to the milliner's shop. There she met a wealthy and elderly Scotsman named McClure, whose conversation consisted of a series of axioms such as "Ignorance is the only devil" and "Man makes his own existence." According to Fanny Mr. McClure had, "after living a tolerably gay life, 'conceived high thoughts, such as Lycurgus loved, who bade flog the little Spartans,' and determined to benefit the species, and immortalise himself, by founding a philosophical school at his Indiana estate. There was something in the hollow square legislations of Mr. Owen that struck him as admirable, and he seems, as far as I can understand, to have intended aiding his views by a sort of incipient hollow square drilling; teaching the young ideas of all he could catch, to shoot into parallelogramic form and order."

What really offended her, however, was that Mr. McClure, after taking over a tract of virgin land and conveying thereto a tremendous number of learned books and scientific instruments, decided that the practical running of the school was a task beneath his dignity and bought an estate in Mexico, leaving his Indiana project in the care of a French woman. "As his acquaintance with this lady had been of long standing, and, as it was said, very intimate," wrote Fanny with asperity, "he felt sure that no violation of his rules would have place under her sway; they would act together as one being: he was to perform the functions of the soul and will everything; she, those of the body, and perform everything."

There was apparently a strict limit to Mr. McClure's philanthropy, for he issued instructions that the expenses of his

venture were to be met out of the profits from the agricultural labours of its students, most of whom were the hefty
sons of poverty-stricken farmers. Since these lads had journeyed long distances to obtain the wonderful free education
advertised and since they had no money with which to return
home, they provided excellent material for the thrifty French
woman and her assistant, who was nastily described by Fanny
as "a nephew-son." Within a very short time all pretence at
intellectual studies or scientific research had been abandoned.
The students were neither more nor less than labourers, the
profits were large, and the soulful Mr. McClure was inordi-
nately pleased with the success of his philosophical experiment.

Fanny thought such exploitation of the young disgraceful.
She expressed her feelings, with heat, to Frances Wright, only
to find, to her dismay, that her idealistic friend thought Mr.
McClure and his educational scheme wholly admirable.
When Mrs. Trollope had a little more experience of the new
world, she declared, she would understand the inadvisability
of giving higher education to the sons of "poor whites." Now
in the case of *Negro* children the matter was entirely different. At Nashoba, for example, the greatest care was taken
over artistic training and the prime duty of every teacher was
to eradicate from the pupil's mind any feeling that he or she
belonged to an inferior race. . . .

But as she listened to the ardent Negrophile the foreboding which had assailed her at the mouth of the Mississippi
crept again into Fanny's mind. Despite Miss Wright's passionate devotion to her chosen cause her speech echoed some
of the sentiments so devastatingly expressed by Mr. McClure,
while her wholesale condemnation of slave-owners did not
ring quite true. Surely, Fanny reasoned with herself, they

weren't *all* so vile! Surely there were *some* Negroes contented with their lot? Involuntarily she remembered the laughing girl in the garden, but for once she curbed her tongue and waited patiently for the oration to end. Afterwards she climbed the stairs to the bedroom she shared with her daughters, undressed quietly, wrapped herself in a dressing-gown and sat for a long time by the window. Such high hopes were centred on the Nashoba experiment. What should she do if they toppled to the ground? They had a certain amount of money with them, but it would not go far in a country where bare necessities were expensive. Then there was the question of health; here Emily coughed in her sleep and a little shudder ran through Fanny. Children were so vulnerable, and who knew what menace lurked in this hot, humid climate? Suddenly the moon came out from behind a cloud and in its light the Mississippi shone bright as silver—a lovely sight yet one which made Fanny, perhaps for the first time in her life, conscious of the fact that she was nearer fifty than forty, that the effort of conquering that shimmering expanse of water was beyond her strength. Then she pulled herself together—it was patently absurd to imagine being beaten by a *river*—and reached for her diary. By the light of a tallow dip she began to write, framing each letter with unusual care:

> This question of the mental equality, or inequality between us, and the Negro care, is one of great interest, and has certainly never yet been fairly tried; and I expect for my children and myself both pleasure and information from visiting Miss Wright's establishment, and watching the success of her experiment.

Such was Fanny's defiant challenge to the Mississippi, to New Orleans, to the whole of North America: and it was something more, a vindication of her own foolhardy action in bringing Henry, Cecilia and Emily half way across the world in search of something which did not exist.

(iii)

Early in January Miss Wright, M. Hervieu and the Trollopes boarded the steam-boat *Belvidere* which was to take them upriver to Memphis. From the customs-shed the vessel looked large, clean and handsome: and Fanny, delighted at the thought of leaving New Orleans, kept telling the children what a good augury it was that they should start the final stage of their journey at the beginning of a new year, and how the boat resembled the floating baths (*les bains Vigier*) she had once seen in Paris. Unfortunately close inspection of the *Belvidere* revealed much that was undesirable. The deck was crowded with Kentucky flat-boat men returning home after depositing their cargoes at New Orleans. The airy dining-saloon had rows of neat little cots ranged under its windows and proved to be the "gentlemen's cabin" to which ladies were only admitted on sufferance at meal-times. Below this was a gloomy apartment which served as sleeping and living quarters for women passengers, and so revolting was its atmosphere that after reproving Emily for wailing that the carpet smelt of sick, Fanny scribbled fiercely in her diary:

> . . . Oh! that carpet! I will not, I may not describe its condition; indeed it requires the pen of a Swift to do it justice. Let no one who wishes to receive agreeable impressions of American manners, commence their travels in a Mississippi steam-boat; for myself, it is with all sincerity I declare, that I would infinitely prefer sharing the apartment of a party of well conditioned pigs to the being confined to its cabin.

[72]

But worse was to follow. Breakfast, dinner and supper had to be eaten in the company of gentlemen who, despite the fact that they addressed each other as general, colonel or major, crammed the food and the blades of their knives into their mouths at the same time, picked their teeth with forks or pen-knives, used round oaths in conversation, and spat continuously into the various receptacles scattered about the floor. The deck being sacred to the Kentuckians (there were two hundred of them, seldom sober and always quarrelsome) the Trollopes spent most of their time sitting on the narrow gallery running round the cabins; but even here their enjoyment of the fresh air was spoiled by the constant shower of sparks and wood-ash which blew down on them from the funnel.

Sometimes the *Belvidere* stopped to take on wood for the engine—a task performed by the Kentuckians as part-payment for their passage. At each halt Fanny hurried her family ashore and galloped them round a cotton or sugar plantation, an ilex or orange grove—*anywhere* that afforded temporary respite from the sights, smells and sounds of the steam-boat; but after they had passed the sweet small town of Natchez standing on its high bluff, the charm of these little excursions palled. There were no more orange trees, palmettos or paw-paws, no more big houses standing guard over rich plantations; there were only the squalid huts of wood-cutters, a few dejected cows and pigs knee-deep in the swamps, occasional men and women with pallid, apathetic faces, and the endless, brooding forest that seemed to push every living thing towards the flat banks of the river.

Fanny's heart sank lower and lower as the *Belvidere* chugged slowly northwards and the gruesome tales told her by other passengers did nothing to relieve her depression. For all her shrewdness, her quick darting wit, her scorn of stupidity, she was an extraordinarily gullible woman at times and she readily believed that the Mississippi forests were infested by bears, that the banks were covered with alligators, that the wood-cutters and their families chose their semi-aquatic existence deliberately in order to make dollars out of the steam-boat companies, that the dollars were all spent on whisky, and that everybody in the region suffered from ague. She even believed a fearsome story (afterwards she recounted it in her book *Domestic Manners of the Americans*) about a husband, wife and five children who arrived exhausted on the river bank and bribed their few neighbours with "ardent spirits" to help them build a log cabin in a single day:

> The wife and five young children were put in possession of their new home, and slept soundly after a long march. Towards daybreak the husband and father was awakened by a faint cry, and looking up, beheld relics of three of his children scattered over the floor, and an enormous crocodile, with several young ones around her, occupied in devouring the remnants of their horrid meal. He looked around for a weapon, but finding none, and aware that unarmed he could do nothing, he raised himself gently on his bed, and contrived to crawl from thence through a window, hoping that his wife, whom he left sleeping, might with the remaining children rest undiscovered till his return. He flew to his nearest neighbour and besought his aid; in less than half an hour two men returned with him, all three well armed; but alas! they were too late! the wife and her two babes lay mangled on their bloody bed. The gorged reptiles fell an easy prey to their assailants, who, upon examining the place, found the hut had been constructed close to the mouth of a large hole, almost a cavern, where the monster had hatched her hateful brood.

In a country where such ghastly tragedies might occur at any moment what mother could face life with equanimity? Certainly not Frances Trollope! Regardless of the exaggera tions and inaccuracies of this cautionary tale she reproached herself bitterly, but too late, on her folly in leaving her native land; and as they neared Memphis so her fear and dislike of America and her inhabitants deepened.

In truth her whole view of America was, and unfortunately remained, a distorted one. In England, had she sought for them, she would have found human beings existing under conditions every bit as deplorable as those of the Mississippi squatters. She would have found also many people with manners even more repugnant than those of her fellow-passengers aboard the *Belvidere*. But in the England of the eighteen-twenties women of assured social position did not move far beyond the confines of their own small circle and for the most part were totally ignorant of how the mass of their fellow-countrymen lived. Fanny therefore believed everything she saw on her river journey to be indigenous to America. To do her justice she struggled hard (in the book she afterwards wrote on her three years' stay) to take a fair view of life in the new world. She failed for two reasons—her innate obstinacy and the snobbishness which imbued the English middle classes of her day.

But during the closing stages of her Mississippi voyage Fanny felt too wretched to do anything except brood over the horrors surrounding her. Despite the torrential rain (did the sun *ever* shine in this lugubrious region?) she sat huddled in her chair on the gallery trying to ignore Miss Wright's panegyrics on Nashoba which rose in a booming crescendo from the cabin below. The last disastrous touch to her misery was provided when, but a few hours short of Memphis, a violent shudder ran through the *Belvidere*.

Immediately the Kentucky colonels crowded the gallery.

"It's a sawyer!" cried one.

"Yes, a snag!" yelled another.

Fanny glowered at their backs. Why not say in simple English that the steamer had collided with an uprooted tree floating downstream instead of using such uncouth words? But the next instant she leapt to her feet as she heard the captain's stentorian shout, "We're aground!"

"Aground?" she demanded, elbowing her way towards him. "Good heavens! and how long shall we stay here?"

"The Lord in His providence can only tell," he returned piously, "but long enough to tire my patience, I expect."

His patience forsooth! thought the indignant Fanny the following morning, as she watched the unavailing efforts of passing steam-boats to draw the *Belvidere* off her mud-bank by means of ropes. It was the patience of his English passengers that mattered, and her temper grew more and more frayed as the day wore on and the boat remained firmly stuck. She rounded on poor Henry when he remarked innocently that he was writing an account of their adventure to his brothers, reprimanded Cecilia and Emily for trifling faults, and scandalised Miss Wright by announcing at the dinner-table that it seemed a thousand pities the Kentucky gentlemen did not adopt the behaviour as well as the titles of the officers met with at St. James's or the Tuileries.

Not until some thirty-six hours had elapsed did an exceptionally large steam-boat throw out grappling irons and succeed in refloating the *Belvidere,* an event which so exhilarated Fanny that she made an entry in her diary about this "vast and mighty thing of life," chivvied the children into finishing their packing, and gazed with positive affection upon the Southern colonels from whom she was about to part. Once away from this vast, sullen river everything would be different, quite, quite different!

Unfortunately Memphis was not reached until midnight. The rain beat down relentlessly and as the Trollopes stepped ashore they were greeted by the news that the journey to the hotel would have to be undertaken on foot, because the town stood on top of a cliff and the new road leading to it could not be completed until the wet season ended. The bobbing lantern held by a guide did little to alleviate the black darkness, the cliff was a steep one, the "new road" a quagmire that drew travellers into its clammy embrace. Cecilia sobbed and Emily screamed with terror as they sank into this muddy bog; Henry's weak lungs gave way under the strain and he was attacked by a violent fit of coughing; Fanny, annoyed by the cheerful advice shouted back by the sure-footed Miss Wright and worried by the plight of her children, finished the ascent on all fours and minus one shoe and both gloves. When they finally trailed into the bare, brightly-lit hall of the hotel they stared at each other in horror—all were coated in glutinous mud from head to foot, Henry's left trouser-leg was ripped from thigh to ankle, Cecilia's face was badly scratched, Emily had lost her thick shawl, her bonnet and both elastic-sided boots, and M. Hervieu looked exactly like a scarecrow.

Only Miss Wright seemed to have survived the ordeal all in one piece and though Fanny's spirits had again sunk to zero she gave grudging admiration to her friend's spirited handling of Mrs. Anderson, the coldly majestic proprietress. Only the best rooms would be tolerated, buckets of hot water must be provided immediately, a substantial meal within the next hour was essential, clothes must be taken away and dried.

The room to which Fanny and her daughters were ushered was a barrack-like apartment. The hotel, she reflected grimly as she superintended the scrubbing of Cecilia and Emily, was about as new as the road, for the plaster on the walls was still damp and the whole place smelt of mortar. However it was decidely better than the *Belvidere;* at least the beds were clean, the food plentiful and savoury. And tomorrow, she thought drowsily as she laid her head on her pillow, they would drive through the forests of Tennessee to Nashoba.

After recent experiences she might have known Nashoba would not be reached so easily. Thanks to the pitiless rain the wooded track was impassable and the party were obliged to remain in the hotel for another twenty-four hours. Fanny consoled herself by saying they needed this breathing-space to repair the garments torn the previous night, but she was extremely put out when Miss Wright vetoed her suggestion that they have meals in a private room. Mrs. Anderson would regard this as a personal affront, she said, and Mrs. Trollope must remember that it was highly necessary she should make the acquaintance of the town's leading citizens, all of whom took their midday meal at the hotel in order to save their wives the trouble of cooking.

"You mean they bring their families with them?" inquired the curious Fanny.

"Oh, no, the mothers and children just have mash and milk at home."

At this pronouncement Fanny's opinion of Southern gentlemen sank even lower than before. "Just like Indian squaws!" she muttered to her friend's retreating back; then gave a violent jump as a Negro maid, wearing a broad grin and carrying an enormous dinner-bell, sidled past Miss Wright in the doorway. Without asking permission the girl shot across the room to the open window where she clanged the bell vigorously. Fanny, standing beside the girl, watched the male inhabitants of Memphis emerge from shops and offices in response to this summons and march stolidly in the direction of the hotel. Only a plaintive reminder from Emily that there would be no food left if they did not hurry caused her to collect her family and hustle them down to the dining-room. Mrs. Anderson graciously waved them to places near her own, a sign of favour somewhat dimmed in Fanny's eyes by sight of William, a manservant she and Miss Wright had engaged in New Orleans, sitting directly opposite to her.

The Trollopes found considerable difficulty in dealing with their heaped platefuls of venison, potatoes and peach sauce. It was partly because of the toughness of the meat and partly because the table, though a gigantic one, had to accommodate nearly fifty people, most of whom, as Fanny expressed it later, "ate with their elbows." (They also, alas, made frequent use of the spittoons placed here and there on the floor.) But Fanny was fortunate enough to have the only conversationalist in Memphis as neighbour. He proved to be the mayor, "a pleasing gentlemanlike man . . . strangely misplaced in a little town on the Mississippi," and he regaled her with glowing accounts of Cincinnati, describing it as the metropolis of the West with the finest situation this side of the Alleghenies. Rather diffidently Fanny explained they were going to settle at Nashoba, whereupon he looked dubious and said that while the Tennessee settlement provided an excellent outlet for the idealistic, lion-hearted Miss Wright he did not think the life there would be suitable for a softly nurtured English lady. Remembering her frugal upbringing, the scrimping and scraping at Keppel Street, the prolonged struggle with the Harrow farm, Fanny bristled. She had, she assured the mayor, much practical experience of agricultural matters; then adroitly drew his attention to the fact that it had actually ceased raining. She and her children wished to explore Memphis and would welcome his directions.

The mayor was delighted to instruct them, but during the afternoon the Trollopes found out there was very little to explore. The town consisted of one long street which zigzagged southwards for about a mile from the Wolf River tributary. Certainly the view of the Mississippi was more attractive than they had expected, for here its great expanse was broken by a long wooded island, and where the street petered into a mere track a square half mile had been cleared as pasture land for horses, cattle and pigs; but behind and beyond either end of Memphis the forest reared frowning, impenetrable, seeming to warn man that his pitiful efforts at civilisation were of no avail against its savage strength. Already in belligerent mood owing to the mayor's remarks about Nashoba, Fanny felt the forest was throwing her a challenge she had to accept. She marched boldly between the tree-boles on its fringe, regardless of her family's whispered reminiscences of Mama's New Orleans expeditions. "Courage and industry," she declaimed as she stumbled along a rough path over which thorny undergrowth straggled, "have braved the forest's warning!"

She was relieved to hear a dutiful chorus of "Yes, Mama," but soon she reached a quick-flowing stream bridged only by the trunk of a tree. And no sooner had she made a precarious crossing than another, and another, watercourse awaited her. At each the tree-trunk was smaller, shakier; at each the stream grew swifter, wider. Finally, a backward glance having assured her the children were not even in sight, she kilted her voluminous skirts and wriggled astride a yet more primitive bridge. Her private thought was of Napoleon on the eve of his departure for Elba; her public reaction was to call, on her arrival at the far side of a torrent which had somehow taken on all the attributes of Niagara, "I think we should return to Mrs. Anderson's hotel."

They returned with difficulty. By the time they had reached the brief haven of Memphis their garments and their tempers were tattered. Henry, Cecilia and Emily thought only and longingly of food, baths, bed: Fanny was unbearably conscious of the forest that had defeated her, the forest that leaned towards her even in Memphis main street and murmured, "Somewhere in the depths of me lies Nashoba."

(*iv*)

Early the following morning the party climbed into a peculiar looking vehicle called a Dearborn and set off on the last stage of their journey. The sky was lowering, the forest track deeply rutted, the air filled with the squawks of the small green parrots that perched dejectedly on every tree; but Fanny's spirits remained determinedly bright until the Negro driver suddenly whipped up his two horses and sent them at a gallop across a crude wooden bridge which swayed so perilously that the carriage nearly overturned into the flooded stream. Remonstrances merely brought the grinning assurance that they were on a "right good road" and had nothing to fear. Half a mile further on, however, they reached a bridge partially swept away by the recent rains, whereupon the philosophical Negro drove right into the river saying the water was "not deep enough to matter." Within two minutes the front wheels were submerged and the frightened horses had kicked the splinter-bar to smithereens.

"I expect," drawled the driver, "you'll best be riding out upon the horses, as we've got into an unhandsome fix here."

"Yes, Jacob," said the maddeningly composed Miss Wright, "that is what we must do."

With a terrific effort Jacob managed to turn the Dearborn round; then one by one its occupants clambered out, straddled a horse and was brought to the shore. All were drenched to the waist, but they had to stand shivering on the bank while Miss Wright and Jacob discussed what was best to do; and by the time it was decided to return to Memphis, Cecilia and Emily were in tears and Fanny was darting anxious glances towards the coughing Henry. When at length they again squeezed themselves into the Dearborn she sat erect and silent in her corner, fearful lest her tongue betray her dark thoughts. Parrots, floods, bareback riding, complete disregard of the value of human life! Was there to be no end to disillusion?

But rose colour invariably tinted Fanny's view and as she sat before Mrs. Anderson's roaring fire three hours later she chirruped happily to her somewhat morose children about the morrow, when the forest streams would be as tinkling brooks and they would journey smoothly, easily, to their goal. Maybe her optimism was heightened by Miss Wright's dramatic departure on horseback for her beloved Nashoba (William afterwards told Fanny that "the lady rode through places that might have daunted the boldest hunter but took it quite easy") but one finds it hard to condone her reference to the depressed forest parrots as those "gay plumaged birds."

Fanny's cheerfulness persisted, despite innumerable bumpings which bruised the flesh and jolted the bones, throughout their second attempt at conquest of the forest. Once more Jacob was their driver and his negotiation of the three-feet-high tree-stumps in their path called forth her admiration. Moreover the sun was shining and under its benison Fanny remarked brightly that it was a thousand pities their driver could not be transported to Bond Street, London, there to deal with traffic problems.

"Mama," interrupted Cecilia, as the Dearborn gave a terrific lurch, "how far is it to Nashoba?"

"Fifteen miles from Memphis," snapped Fanny. "We should reach it at any moment."

The Doubtful Traveller

Scarcely had she spoken the words than the carriage halted and Jacob's grinning face appeared at the window. "Here we be, ma'am," he said, opening the door with a flourish.

Fanny jumped up, but she paused with one foot on the step. In her most despondent moods she had not imagined such a melancholy scene as that which now presented itself. A half-hearted attempt had been made at clearing the forest and in every direction stretched a sea of mud. Out of this rose grotesque, leafless trees surrounded by crazy palings, and at intervals rough log cabins squatted in the brown ooze, looking for all the world like enormous toads.

"I guess you'll have to lep," said the philosophic Jacob, "there ain't no path yet."

The Trollopes "lepped" obediently—fortunately there were innumerable tree-stumps to serve as stepping-stones—urged on by glad cries from Miss Wright, who had appeared in the doorway of the nearest cabin. "Welcome to Nashoba!" she called, and to Fanny, teetering on a slimy stump between leaps, it seemed the most idiotic remark she had ever heard.

On completing their hazardous journey they were greeted by Miss Wright's sister Camilla and her husband, both of whom shivered as with ague and looked wretchedly ill. "It's the climate," shuddered Camilla, helping them off with their wraps, "so—so d-d-damp."

In a booming aside Miss Wright assured Fanny that her sister and brother-in-law were "poor things." Food would be brought shortly, she added; meanwhile she would whisk Henry and Hervieu off to their quarters and leave Mrs. Trollope and the girls to settle cosily into their cabin—the *best* one on the estate.

When she had gone Fanny looked around in dismay. The cabin consisted of two rooms furnished with the barest necessities and filled with the acrid smoke that belched from the primitive fireplace. A chill wind whistled through the gaps in the log walls, the mattresses appeared to be stuffed with bricks, the supply of blankets was meagre. Cecilia and Emily sat on a wooden bench she dragged close to the fire. When was supper coming? Where had Henry gone? How long were they going to stay in this awful place?

"Don't ask stupid questions," said Fanny, sucking her thumb. (The home-made furniture bristled with splinters.) "And do, I beg of you, stop snuffling." But even as she spoke her doubts about Nashoba resolved themselves into a fierce dislike of everybody and everything in the settlement, a dislike which developed during the next twenty-four hours into actual hatred.

It must be admitted there was plenty of fuel to feed her wrath. Comfort was non-existent. At each meal they were served with bowls of Indian corn porridge accompanied by hunks of fried fat pork, a monotonous diet which did unconscionable things to Trollopian stomachs. The only evidence of the much-vaunted school lay in the piles of mouldering primers and textbooks stacked up in odd corners. Apart from the Wright contingent there were some thirty to forty Negroes, including children, who seemed to spend their days standing dejectedly in the mud staring at their surroundings. Camilla and her husband seized every opportunity to embark on an account of the dire ailments caused by the rains and mists of the winter and by the flies, mosquitoes and humidity of the summer; while Frances delivered an endless oration on the professors she had engaged (they were eagerly awaiting the start of their stupendous educational experiment), the wonderful crops of cotton and Indian corn the clearing had yielded the previous year, the large number of slaves clamouring for entry to the settlement, the uplifting effect of the beauties of nature on the human mind.

Fanny surveyed the Negroes, the mud, the food, the cabins, the shivering Camilla, the close-packed forest trees standing all around like sentinels, and promptly decided she did not believe one word of her friend's speech. Certainly the rain had ceased and the patch of sky visible above the clearing was a vivid blue, but somehow this served only to emphasise the sheer misery of the scene. As for the forest, peer as she might she could discern no opening in it, no vista along which one might gaze at a sunlit glade, and the longer she looked the more she realised the implacable enmity of this barrier between her and the outside world. Not so long ago she had vowed she would conquer the Mississippi River: now she acknowledged defeat at the hands of its counterpart, the Mississippi forest.

To reveal such a humiliating situation was out of the question, so she indulged in a series of verbal fencing-bouts with Miss Wright. Of course Nashoba was a magnificent experiment assured of success, but didn't her friend think that in its present-er-primitive condition it was not quite the place in which to bring up Cecilia and Emily? Then there was Henry's delicate chest to be considered—he was so susceptible to climate, poor boy. Perhaps later on when the school and agricultural activities were in full swing it might be possible for them to return? In reply Miss Wright graciously agreed that the girls must naturally miss the luxuries to which they were accustomed and that the climate might prove too harsh for a boy suffering from lung trouble. As for returning at some later date, she felt sure that her dear Mrs. Trollope would understand she already had a long waiting-list.

On the surface both ladies were exquisitely polite; but an alert observer could have discerned Miss Wright's indignation at the lack of idealistic fervour in the Trollope family and Fanny's resentment at having been so grossly misled. It was arranged, with many protestations of mutual regret, that the visitors should leave in ten days' time. The night before her departure Fanny wrote in her diary:

> One glance sufficed to convince me that every idea I had formed of the place [Nashoba] was as far as possible from the truth. Desolation was the only feeling—the only word that presented itself; but it was not spoken. I think, how-ever, that Miss Wright was aware of the painful impression the sight of her forest home produced on me, and I doubt not that the conviction reached us both at the same moment, that we had erred in thinking that a few months passed to-gether at this spot could be productive of pleasure to either. But to do her justice, I believe her mind was so exclusively occupied by the object she had then in view, that all things else were worthless, or indifferent to her. I never heard or read of any enthusiasm approaching hers, except in some instances, in ages past, or religious fanaticism.

Apart from the dig in the last sentence, doubtless inspired by Miss Wright's unkind reference to Henry's lungs, this un-usually restrained entry shows how deeply Nashoba affected Fanny; it shows also awareness of her own failure to demand factual details of the place before crossing the Atlantic.

Frances Wright pointedly refrained from inquiring about the Trollopes' destination—she was seriously upset by Au-guste Hervieu's last-minute decision to throw in his lot with them—but in the bustle of departure Camilla asked if they proposed to return to England. "No," said Fanny, "we think we shall settle in Cincinnati, the metropolis of the West. I learn from an American friend that it has the finest situation this side of the Alleghenies." Then she threw back her head and looked boldly at the forest: "I am told the woods sur-rounding the town are renowned for their enchanting vistas."

Five minutes later she bade farewell to a sorely puzzled

Camilla and stepped spryly into the Dearborn. When Jacob whipped up his horses she leaned far forward in her seat, as if to urge their progress. There were no backward glances, no affectionate wavings of the hand, no protestations of regret. Before Memphis was reached Fanny had erased all memory of Nashoba from her mind. Another odyssey had begun.

Trollope's Folly

1828-1831

(*i*)

THE party arrived back at Anderson's hotel in blithe mood. After the derelict cabins of Nashoba its bare mortar-smelling rooms appeared palatial, while its inhabitants—even to the awe-inspiring proprietress herself—welcomed them with a warmth which suggested they had been snatched by some miracle from the very jaws of death. Everything, thought Fanny a trifle sententiously, was comparative. A fortnight earlier she had found Memphis a depressing place: now it looked clean, bright, civilised; the dawns and sunsets were superb, and in some mysterious way the inimical forest seemed to have shrunk in size.

The news that they would have to wait five days for the Cincinnati steam-boat delighted the young Trollopes, whose experiences over the past three months had taught them gratitude for small mercies. Now that he was no longer absorbed in his dreams of teaching art to the downtrodden slaves of the Mississippi basin, Auguste Hervieu proved an amusing and intelligent companion and with him they wandered happily through the little town, their especial joy being to watch the constant river traffic and the loading and unloading of ships on the quays below the cliff.

For once the energetic Fanny did not accompany her family on these expeditions. Her time was fully occupied in the composition of long thoughtful letters to Thomas Anthony, urging him to join them in Cincinnati. True, she had not yet seen that city herself but she was only too well aware that desperate measures were required to solve immediate problems. So far the American venture had been costly and in vain. Her stock of money was rapidly dwindling. A job had to be found for Henry and some sort of education provided for Cecilia and Emily, while on the other side of the Atlantic Ocean her sick, harassed husband struggled to cope with two farms and the growing needs of Thomas Adolphus and Anthony. Faced with a situation one tenth as precarious the strongest might have quailed—and it must be remembered too that the grievous wound dealt by Nashoba was still open and throbbing.

Fanny's over-impulsiveness had led her to embark too rashly on a project which her common sense should have told her was bound to fail. But in all fairness it must be acknowledged that she was by no means the only person to be spellbound by Miss Wright's eloquence and that to her the sudden destruction of all her hopes meant much more than it would have done to most people; therefore her courage in determining to build an entirely fresh life for her husband and children in Ohio fell little short of the sublime. Indeed it is hard to imagine any other woman of her day attempting such a task; yet so resilient was she that her letters to Thomas Anthony rang with confidence. Everyone spoke of Cincinnati's beauty, riches and incredible prosperity. . . . They said it was the coming city of America, called it variously the "wonder of the west," the "prophet's gourd of magic growth,' the "infant Hercules". . . . So intriguing were the accounts of this earthly paradise that she and the children felt they shared the excitement of Rousseau's novice, *"un voyage à faire, et Paris en bout!"* . . . So soon as he received these comments would he hasten to join them in the speediest possible manner? . . . Meanwhile she would find a suitable home and a post for Henry. . . .

And as she turned from her writing to greet the son and daughters who came in full of the day's adventures Fanny's heart glowed with pride. They looked so cheerful, so eager, Henry seemed stronger already, the girls' cheeks actually had a trace of sunburn. Ah, how happy they were going to be! In the beneficent Ohio air Thomas Anthony's headaches would disappear and soon, very soon, they would be affluent enough to send for Thomas Augustus and Anthony.

Then came news that the *Criterion* had arrived. According to Fanny, "the company on board was wonderfully like what we had met in coming from New Orleans; I think they must have all been first cousins; and what was singular, they too had all arrived at high rank in the army," but she was so relieved at the thought of leaving the muddy waters and swampy shores of the Mississippi that this time she ignored these military gentlemen and scurried over her meals in order to return to her seat by the guard rail in case she missed the approach to *La Belle Rivière*. Nor did the Ohio disappoint her when it was reached. Its clear waters sparkled in the sunlight as they flowed through rolling open country sweeter and more homely than she had yet seen. Certainly the primeval forest seemed reluctant to forsake the scene altogether and at intervals the giant trees clung tenaciously to high bluffs, but for the most part green meadows bordered the banks while every few miles there were settlements with neat, gaily painted little houses perched beside silvery waterfalls.

Pleasant though it was to watch this smiling landscape from *Criterion's* deck Fanny soon grew restless and insisted upon going ashore when they stopped to refuel, a decision which brought her renewed qualms as the settlers to whom she talked were yellow-skinned, emaciated folk full of melancholy tales of relations who had "lately died of the fever." The thought that departure from the Mississippi had not brought escape from the "mephitic air" brooding over its shores was a disturbing one and Fanny kept an anxious eye on Henry. Again, when a day was spent in Louisville and she was so impressed by its cleanliness and lovely surroundings that she almost decided to settle there instead of Cincinnati, she was told that during the summer the inhabitants died like flies. There were, it seemed, still serpents in Eden, but she did her best to put these out of mind and by dint of arguing with a Kentucky colonel about shiftless methods of husbandry (the poor man had never heard of the rotation of crops) she nearly succeeded by the time they reached their destination on February 10th.

First view of Cincinnati was exhilarating. Around the paved landing-stage that stretched a full quarter-mile were set large solid buildings. The town itself was arranged neatly on the southern slope of a hill and was sheltered from the north winds by higher, wooded hills; many of the houses were three-storied and there was actually a church with two small spires. Without perhaps realising it the Trollopes had been yearning for sight of bricks and mortar. They gazed on Cincinnati and were awed by its splendour.

The hour being noon they hurried to the Washington Hotel, but recoiled on entering the dining-room, for the male habit of eating out seemed yet more popular here than in Memphis and the room was packed to suffocation. A kindly waitress with an Irish brogue then ushered them into the "bar-room," which was occupied by several of the town's more emancipated wives from whom Fanny immediately asked particulars of local house agents. Oblivious alike of their stilted replies, dark looks and remarks about foreigners she galloped through her meal. It was imperative to find a house *at once,* if only in order to eat in privacy.

With the family and Hervieu at her heels she sallied forth and interviewed a most amenable gentleman who not only assured her he had plenty of houses at reasonable rentals but suggested his boy should escort them as guide. Up one street and down another he led them until Fanny demanded how long this pilgrimage was going to last. He explained that he was looking for "to let" bills in the windows and when Fanny remonstrated with the boy he started knocking on each door they passed, inquiring if the owners were willing to vacate their homes, a process which so outraged Fanny that she told him to go back to his master. In return he shouted abuse, saying he was entitled to a dollar fee, and it took the combined efforts of Henry and Hervieu to get rid of him while a flustered but undefeated Fanny marched ahead with the girls. It was now her turn to look for bills in windows and by great good fortune she shortly spied one. The house it advertised was on the small side, but compact and seemingly well-built, and the landlord was an obliging man who promised to tidy the place up so that they could move in the next day.

Tired but happy they trailed back to the Washington, where Fanny told the Irish waitress to serve tea for all of them in her bedroom. "Och, my honey," said the woman, "ye'll be from the old country. I'll see you will have your tay all to yourselves, honey," and presently she staggered upstairs bearing a huge tray. Besides tea there were pieces of "hung beef, 'chipped up' raw, and sundry sweetmeats of brown sugar hue and flavour" which proved much more appetising than they looked. They were all chattering nineteen-to-the-dozen about the new house when a loud knock came at the door and the burly landlord entered.

"Are any of you ill?"

"No, thank you sir," said Fanny politely, "we are all quite well."

"Then, madam," he replied in a dictatorial voice, "I must tell you that I cannot accommodate you on these terms; we have no family tea-drinkings here, and you must live either with me and my wife, or not at all in this house."

Fanny was so taken aback that her usual quickness of tongue deserted her and she murmured confusedly that being strangers they were unaccustomed to American manners.

"Our manners are very good manners," barked the landlord, "and we don't wish any changes from England."

Secure in the knowledge that they were leaving in the morning Fanny told him tartly he would not be troubled by English habits much longer; but afterwards she wrote, "I thought of mine host of the Washington when reading Scott's *Anne of Geierstein;* he, in truth, strongly resembled the inn-keeper therein immortalised, who made his guests eat, drink and sleep, just where, when, and how he pleased."

(*ii*)

Fanny awakened early on February third, to a delicious feeling of well-being. At last, after the innumerable vicissitudes they had suffered since leaving England, she and the children were in a home of their own again. So entrancing was the knowledge that for a few minutes she lay relaxed, her gaze wandering idly round the room. Although the

furniture was ugly it was at least serviceable. There was no
carpet on the floor—an American habit which seemed very
strange to her. Still, the whole house would look very
different when her own goods and chattels were installed.
How wise she had been to ignore Miss Wright's advice to
travel as light as possible! Here she chuckled remembering
that lady's shocked glance at her retort that if Lord Byron
had been able to transport his four-poster bed across Europe
she could surely take a few rugs, pictures and chairs across
the Atlantic. . . . Suddenly her glance lit on the window
blinds and she frowned slightly. Just imagine using *wall
paper* for blinds, rolling and unrolling the wretched thing
morning and night, balancing on a ladder trying to fasten
them to the window-frames with bits of string! Making a
mental note to speak to the landlord about this awkward
arrangement she rose, dressed and went downstairs to pre
pare breakfast.

Now Fanny was no stranger to household chores, but never
had she had to cook a meal under such difficulties. The
wood-burning stove was a most primitive affair, and the fuel
was green. She searched the house for a water tank; she
searched the yard for a pump; and she found neither. There
were no pots or kettles; the silver, cutlery and china had to
be unpacked; and she was almost frantic when a small child
carrying an empty jug knocked on the door with the astonish
ing announcement that "the cow was not come home, and i
was too late to look for her to breakfast now." By question
ing she elicited the horrifying information that most of the
poorer families kept a cow. This beast wandered where i
listed, returning home only at night and morning when i
stood outside the house and devoured a large tubful of
Indian corn mess while it was being milked. Occasionally
as in this case, the cow found a more succulent repast in the

ields or (dreadful thought!) the town gutters, and failed to keep its appointment.

In the end the Trollopes breakfasted on fruit; then Henry was sent to ask the landlord to call and the others tackled the task of unpacking. By midday the house was beginning to look more homey, but the kitchen quarters were knee-deep in papers and shavings and Fanny's list of things to ask the landlord had grown ominously long. He arrived when the family were eating boiled eggs (the girls had visited the market and Hervieu had staggered gallantly from a near-by stream with buckets of water) and did not show the least concern over his tenant's complaints, drawling monosyllabic answers and prefacing each remark with the words "old woman." He'd never heard tell of folk using anything but wallpaper for blinds. Cincinnati didn't hold with cisterns or pumps; why should they with so much water around? They didn't consider drains were necessary either; they'd done a hard enough job making a fine city out of bear-infested cane-brake in a short thirty years. The only time he displayed any animation was when the exasperated Fanny waved at the packing litter and asked when the dustman's cart came round.

What was wrong, he demanded, with those two young men making a bonfire of the stuff! As for ordinary house refuse— he drew himself upright and addressed his tenant severely: "Your Help will just have to fix them all into the middle of the street, but you must mind, old woman, that it is the middle. I expect you don't know as we have got a law what forbids throwing such things at the sides of the streets; they must just all be cast right into the middle, and the pigs soon takes them off."

The dazed Fanny clutched at the only word in this speech

which seemed to carry a gleam of hope. A Help! Wher
and how soon could she find such a treasure?

The landlord relapsed into indifference. The young girl
preferred to work in the paper-mills or other factories. Sh
might get a free Negro, of course—plenty of those lived i
the quarter known as Little Africa; or she might find some
one from an outlying farm. . . . But as he spoke he edged ou
of the doorway. It was clear he thought he had done enough
for these awkward strangers.

In the next week, however, the Trollopes discovere
kinder hearts. Various neighbours called with help an
advice, and though they were rough-mannered women wh
persisted in calling her "honey" Fanny was exceedingl
grateful for their generous aid. They explained that th
only actual shops in the city were bakeries and that all othe
foodstuffs were bought in the market, which it was advisabl
to visit before breakfast as it was pretty well over by eigh
o'clock. She should not, they said, pay more than four cent
(twopence) the pound for good beef or veal, twelve cent
for poultry trussed ready for table or half that if bough
alive, and fifty cents for geese or turkeys. Mutton was in
ferior, but the Ohio provided good cheap fish, and vegetable
—particularly tomatoes and many kinds of bean—wer
abundant.

Fanny found it odd at first to leave home with a large
basket soon after dawn, but the fine quality and low price
of food delighted her and she was extremely relieved when
one of her new friends introduced her to a farmer who no
only pastured his cattle properly but delivered milk each
morning. On the whole she settled down quickly to a way
of life which would have appalled her six months earlier
but three things continued to worry her and two of them
alas, had to be endured for the whole of her stay in Cincin

nati. One was the complete lack of drainage, for since the town was built on a hillside with the main streets and factory district close to the river the frequent heavy showers washed all the refuse from the higher streets with the result that a stream of filthy black liquid trickled downhill to settle into a glutinous mass on the uneven sidewalks of the lower town. Assailed by memories of the typhoid which had attacked Thomas Adolphus and Henry in Harrow, Fanny protested vigorously that this deposit was bound to produce miasma in the warm weather. Anyone of common sense knew that public hygiene was necessary to health, and thanks to the situation of the place the construction of proper drains was the simplest matter in the world. She was right—but her vehement expositions did nothing to endear her to Cincinnati's citizens.

Outspoken comments on her second worry brought her into even greater disfavour. The majority of the townsfolk made their living out of hogs. They bred them, killed them, ate them, bought and sold them. The local newspaper was filled with such advertisements as, "Wanted, immediately, 4,000 fat hogs," or "For sale, 2,000 barrels of prime pork," and the porcine population of Cincinnati was far larger than the human one. Since it was stupid to waste good corn mess on animals that preferred garbage the hogs were allowed to roam the town at will and, although Fanny was heard to say it was "well they were so numerous and so active in their capacity of scavengers, for without them the streets would soon be choked up with all sorts of substances in every stage of decomposition," she was never forgiven for her further remarks (afterwards put into her book):

> If I determined upon a walk up Main Street, the chances were five hundred to one against my reaching the shady side without brushing by a snout fresh dripping from the

kennel; when we had screwed our courage to the enterprise of mounting a certain noble-looking sugar-loaf hill, that promised pure air and a fine view, we found the brook we had to cross, at its foot, red with the stream from a pig slaughter-house; while our noses, instead of meeting "the thyme that loves the green hill's breast," were greeted by odours that I will not describe, and which I heartily hope my readers cannot imagine; our feet, that on leaving the city had expected to press the flowery sod, literally got entangled in pigs' tails and jaw-bones: and thus the prettiest walk in the neighbourhood was interdicted for ever.

Her third worry, that of obtaining a Help, speedily assumed monstrous proportions in her mind, for while she was an excellent housewife she simply could not cope unaided with marketing, cooking, cleaning and the hundred extra chores which had to be done thanks to primitive conditions. Besides, she had come to Cincinnati to seek prosperity for them all, not to hew wood and draw water. There was Henry's career to think of, and the girls' education, and some sort of business to be found that would suit Thomas Anthony and herself. But how could she tackle these problems when she was literally chained to the kitchen?

She was delighted therefore when one morning a stately young woman appeared and said, "I be come to help you."

Fanny, aware that the word "servant" was frowned upon but otherwise ignorant of the correct procedure, began the usual catechism through which one put maids in England by asking what yearly wage she required.

To her amazement the girl roared with laughter. "Oh Gimini! You be a downright Englisher, sure enough. I should like to see a young lady engage by the year in America! I hope I shall get a husband before many months, or I expect I shall be an outright old maid, for I be most seventeen already; besides, mayhap I may want to go to school. You must just give me a dollar and half a week, and mother's slave, Phillis, must come over once a week, I expect, from t'other side the water, to help me clean."

A Help was a Help, so Fanny restrained her tongue with difficulty and meekly agreed to the girl's demands. When she found, however, that she was preparing to start work forthwith in a yellow dress embroidered with red roses, she suggested she should change as it was a shame to spoil such a fine gown.

" 'Tis just my best and my worst," said the young woman carelessly, "for I've got no other."

It turned out she had no luggage of any kind, a fact which so horrified Fanny that she gave her money to buy under-clothes and other essentials and promptly cut out some material which Cecilia and Emily made up into a dress. The Help grinned with pleasure when it was finished but instead of thanking them demanded the loan of bonnets, shawls and trinkets to wear on her outings. Rather sharply Fanny refused, whereupon the girl drawled: "Well, I never seed such grumpy folks as you be; there is several young ladies of my acquaintance what goes to live out now and then with the old women about the town, and they and their girls always lends them what they asks for; I guess you English thinks we should poison your things, just as bad as if we was Negurs." Her work was of the slap-dash variety and when, after a handful of weeks, Fanny said she could not lend her money to buy a silk ball-dress she walked out with the remark, "Then 'tis not worth my while to stay any longer!"

So once again Fanny cried "Help!" to everyone within reach and in a few days two pretty sisters presented themselves. One was thoroughly soured because she had to earn her living in what she considered a degrading way; for had she not been told a thousand times that she was as good as any other lady, that all men were equal, and women too, and that it was a sin and a shame for a free-born American to be treated like a servant? She went hungry rather than eat in the kitchen, spent most of her time in tears on her bed and finally departed with the ominous warning, "I expect you'll see no more of me." Her sister, less concerned with the rights of man, stayed on until she had amassed, by fair and foul means, an extensive wardrobe from Cecilia and Emily.

Fanny was at her wits' end and when a solemn-faced girl called Nancy Fletcher turned up with a bundle of clothing and a hideous story of a childhood passed among cruel step-mothers, thieving brothers and faithless sweethearts, she accepted her without demur. Nancy proved an excellent worker (a welcome change) and beguiled her tasks by recounting how she had "got religion." This was such a comfort to her that she craved permission to go to Meeting every Tuesday and Thursday. "You shall not have to want me, Mrs. Trollope, for our minister knows that we have all our duties to perform to man, as well as to God, and he makes the Meeting late in the evening that they may not cross one another."

Her request was readily agreed to; indeed Fanny was charmed with this "second Jeanie Deans" who worked like a Trojan, read a passage from the Bible each day, and had triumphed so nobly over her early troubles. True, she once remonstrated with her about coming in late at night, but Nancy's grave reply made her feel almost ashamed. "Oh, Mrs. Trollope, I am late indeed! We have this night had seventeen souls added to our flock. May they live to bless this night!"

But to the family's deep distress Nancy fell very sick. For days life was despaired of and Fanny nursed her devotedly, noticing that even in delirium her thoughts seemed to ramble to heaven, and soothing her when she kept repeating, "I have been a sinner, but I am safe in the Lord Jesus." On her recovery she said she must have a change of air and begged the loan of three dollars for her holiday. Unfortunately a lady called during her absence and inquired agitatedly if she were in the house. On being told she was away she exclaimed, "Thank God! Never let her enter your doors again, she is the most abandoned woman in the town: a gentleman who knows you, has been told that she lives with you, and that she boasts of having the power of entering your house at any hour of the night."

Almost without volition Fanny's mind went back to the evening when seventeen souls were saved and she listened with growing alarm to a long account of Nancy's iniquities. Just to think she had housed such a dangerous character under the same roof as her innocent children! The girl was due to return next evening and she passed the interval "meditating how to get rid of her without an *eclaircissement*." To her relief Nancy denied nothing and gave them all wide smiles as she left, but Fanny wrote later, "This adventure frightened me so heartily that, notwithstanding, I had the dread of cooking my own dinner before my eyes, I would not take any more young ladies into my family without receiving some slight sketch of their former history."

Since any requests for references were strongly resented by Cincinnati Help she had to cook her own dinners for quite a long time. Eventually, however, she managed to find a most competent Frenchwoman, and soon afterwards a nice English girl, to assist her. These two remained with the Trollopes until shortly before they left the town, lifting at least one worry from Fanny's over-burdened shoulders.

(*iii*)

Despite all her early domestic troubles Fanny insisted from the very beginning of their stay that some semblance of social and cultural life must be maintained. At the first opportunity she visited a school kept by a Dr. Lock, "a gentleman who appeared to have liberal and enlarged opinions on the subject of female education." Here the young ladies of Cincinnati enrolled for "a quarter's" mathematics, or "two quarters' " political economy, moral philosophy, algebra and quadratic equations, after which they were automatically awarded a diploma. Fanny was privileged to listen to a blushing and obviously bewildered sixteen year old being examined in moral philosophy and her subsequent comments were not appreciated by Dr. Lock. She said rightly that a short period of cramming, however intensive, could not enable a hitherto ignorant girl to attain eminence in any of the higher branches of science and added that she thought the choice of subjects singularly unsuitable for scholars whose destiny would be the bearing and tending of half a score of children with the doubtful aid of one Help.

Cincinnati held many other schools, but the afternoon spent at Dr. Lock's establishment was enough for Fanny. Busy as she was she found time to instruct Cecilia and Emily in English literature, needlework and dressmaking. Henry taught them history and the rudiments of arithmetic while Hervieu was only too glad to return his hostess' kindness by giving them French lessons. Thus the problem of the girls' education was solved and their energetic parent moved on to the making of social contacts, contacts without which life would be bleak indeed.

In England, as we know, Fanny had been an excellent hostess around whom guests young and old, gay and erudite, had eagerly flocked: in Cincinnati she found, to her dismay, that the American idea of an "At Home" or a reception was the exact opposite of her own and that when she entertained people were liable to regard her as some sort of freak. She delighted in stimulating conversation and the introducing of guests to each other, in the serving of dainty little titbits, in serious discussion of music, painting or literature. The Cincinnatians believed in the giving of enormous evening parties at which the women herded at one end of the drawing-room and the men at the other. "The gentlemen spit," wrote Fanny acidly, "talk of elections and the price of produce, and spit again. The ladies look at each other's dresses till they know every pin by heart; talk of Parson Somebody's last sermon on the day of judgment, or Dr. T'otherbody's new pills for dyspepsia, till the 'tea' is announced, when they all console themselves together for whatever they may have suffered in keeping awake, by taking more tea, coffee, hot cake and custard, hoe cake, johnny cake, waffle cake and dodger cake, pickled peaches, preserved cucumbers, ham, turkey, hung beef, apple sauce and pickled oysters than ever were prepared in any other country of the known world."

These parties—and they were invited to at least two each week—tried the Trollopes sorely, particularly Fanny. She readily admitted that it was difficult for women who, however wealthy, had to spend their days in household drudgery to appear as elegant and sparkling companions in the evening, but she did feel they might display a modicum of intelligence. Nor could she accustom herself to the male habit of giving lavish card, music, dinner or supper parties from which all women were strictly excluded. She was sure it was responsible for the odious way gentlemen chewed tobacco and spat on every conceivable occasion. But behind and beyond these personal criticisms she was uncomfortably aware of what she termed "the national feeling of, I believe, unconquerable dislike, which evidently lives at the bottom of every truly American heart, against the English."

Her view may have been coloured by her own dislike of Cincinnati (for the first fine careless rapture lived but briefly) but certainly she had to listen time and again to remarks which, if comical, were also irritating. One lady said smugly that she supposed the British Government "must just be fit to hang themselves for that last war they cooked up; it has been the ruin of you, I expect, for it has just been the making of us." Another announced graciously, "Well, I do begin to understand your broken English better than I did . . . for everybody knows that London slang is the most dreadful in the world," while a third asked solemnly if the Trollopes had left home to escape the vermin with which the English of all ranks were afflicted.

Fortunately Fanny's sense of humour had not atrophied in the mephitic airs of the Mississippi and she was highly entertained by these statements and even more so by a conversation held with someone to whom she had just been introduced.

"Don't you hate chintzes, Mrs. Trollope?"

Fanny blinked. "No, indeed, I think them very pretty."

"There now!" exclaimed the lady, "if that is not being English! I reckon you call that loving your country; well, thank God, we Americans have something better to love our country for than that comes to; we are not obliged to say that we like nasty filthy chintzes to show that we are good patriots!"

"Chintzes?" burst out Fanny, "what *are* chintzes?"

"Possible! Do you pretend you don't know what chintzes are? Why, the nasty little stinking blood-suckers that all the beds in London are full of."

It was only later that the bewildered Fanny discovered that the word "bug," used by her American friends to describe practically any insect, was not applied to the "unfortunate cosmopolite known by that name amongst us." Instead it was referred to by the Spanish word *chinche*.

But amusing as Fanny found such interludes she was seriously perturbed by the lack of congenial companionship for her young folks. As the spring advanced (and an as yet unmasked Nancy Fletcher toiled in the kitchen) she gave a few small music parties, the guests being curly-haired youths in fancy waistcoats and sweet shy girls who hid the rolls of music they had brought under their wraps. In vain did Fanny chatter brightly of famous singers, violinists, pianists and orchestras she had heard; in vain did she coax Miss A. or Miss B. to display their talents. The girls blushed and giggled, the youths muttered to each other in a corner, everyone shunned the piano like the plague and the sole topic of conversation was, "How many quarters' music have you had?" There was no doubt about it, the parties were a dead failure. Perhaps, she thought sadly, she hadn't provided enough waffle or dodger cake? But picnics now, surely picnics would prove popular?

They did not. When their sons and daughters received Fanny's politely worded invitations the scandalised matrons of Cincinnati descended on the Englishwoman in a body. They should not dream of allowing their offspring to walk all that way in the midday heat along a road in which a public-house was situated to a part of the forest everybody knew was infested by frogs, lizards, locusts, katydids, beetles, hornets and mosquitoes—there followed a list of the dread diseases such foolhardy travellers were bound to develop. Besides, here the deputation lowered their voices, did not Mrs. Trollope realise it was considered *very* indelicate for ladies and gentlemen to sit down together on the grass?

After that Fanny abandoned the social education of young Cincinnati in despair. In future, she declared, the family would seek their own diversions in the museums, art galleries and lecture halls which the city seemed to possess in abundance. They began with a visit to a natural history museum which proved to be neither more nor less than a waxworks show, but on their second expedition were fortunate in finding a similar museum belonging to a Mr. Dorfeuille, a scientist of repute, who had a collection of most interesting Indian antiquities. In order to attract custom, however, he too had resorted to wax figures. An upper floor of his house contained a sort of Chamber of Horrors. There were mechanical dwarfs that grew into giants as one watched them, ebony imps with fire darting from their eyeballs, huge snakes in the act of swallowing beautiful maidens, all these exhibits being viewed through a massive iron grating cunningly connected by wires with an electrical machine in the background. Any spectator (and few could resist the impulse) who put hand or foot between the bars received a smart shock which often passed from one to another of the crowd causing shrieks of terror. To the Cincinnatians "Dorfeuille's Hell" was a place of very real horror: to the Trollopes it was one of the most amusing exhibitions imaginable.

The municipal picture gallery proved a bitter disappointment as young Hervieu had built such high hopes on the city's interest in art. The paintings were the merest daubs, the lighting was poor, the only patrons a handful of school-children playing hide and seek round groups of exceedingly bad statuary. But as Fanny quickly pointed out this was all to the good because it gave Hervieu an unrivalled opportunity to educate public taste in the way it should go. So eloquent did she wax that he hurried off with the sketches he had made of his proposed picture of General Lafayette's landing to show them to some leading merchants, and these gentlemen introduced him to a German drawing-master who immediately offered him a post in his school at a salary of five hundred dollars a year.

Naturally there were great rejoicings over this appointment, for they had all grown attached to the young Frenchman; moreover, Fanny thought it an excellent omen for Henry's future. They must, she said, identify themselves more with the educational side of the city life (she had forgotten Dr. Lock) and to this end she took tickets for a lecture on phrenology by a Dr. Caldwell, who was billed as the "Spurzheim of America." The packed hall was evidence that the Cincinnatians were aching for intellectual sustenance and if Fanny found some of the lecturer's utterances a trifle woolly perhaps it was because she had listened to the famous Spurzheim himself. Her enthusiasm rose again when the audience declared their intention of forming a Phrenological Society and proceeded to do so in most business-like fashion, electing office-bearers and registering a large number of potential subscribers. The first meeting was crowded, the second meeting was attended by about fifty people who drowsed and chewed alternately while those on the platform passed resolutions "sufficient to fill three folios." For the third meeting, at which subscriptions were to be paid, the treasurer and Fanny arrived punctually and sat staring at each other for two hours as they waited patiently but vainly for the "wise men of the west."

Fanny was justifiably annoyed, but when Henry and Hervieu said they were not surprised she retorted that nobody could expect people whose lives centred round hogs, bear-brake and Mr. Dorfeuille's Chamber of Horrors to turn suddenly towards learned pursuits; they had to be led step by step in the right direction. Meanwhile she felt they should give their support to the theatre and induce friends to join them as she had met the managers, Mr. and Mrs. Alexander Drake, and formed a high opinion of their efforts to interest the citizens in Shakespeare's plays.

The theatre was small and dirty, the seating arrangements uncomfortable, but the Drakes were uncommonly fine actors, she a tragedienne and he a comedian, and they worked like heroes. What hurt Fanny was that the audience (who should have been listening breathless to the immortal lines) lay back on their posteriors with their feet cocked on the back of the seat in front, chewed, spat, ate raw onions, gave vent to unearthly yells by way of applause, and bawled "Yankee Doodle" whenever some "foreign" phrase made them feel extra patriotic. To make matters worse the occasional performances of modern plays by fifth-rate touring companies always drew a full house and behaviour which, by comparison, was excellent. Despite the assiduous attendance of the Trollope family and their lavish praise of the Drakes, Cincinnati remained distressingly oblivious to Shakeaspeare's genius and even Fanny had become a shade cynical about her American friends' mental powers before an event occurred which roused a variety of emotions in her breast.

Returning from market one morning she was stopped by acquaintance after acquaintance who said, round-eyed, "Have you heard the news? Miss Wright, of Nashoba, is

going to lecture at the court-house!" The whole of Main
Street buzzed with talk, partly because people had heard
garbled and derogatory reports of Frances Wright's "mad
ideas about niggers." but principally because it was entirely
unknown for a rich and well-born lady so to demean herself
as to give a public lecture. Furthermore she was going to
speak on "The Nature of True Knowledge" and would be
sure to propound the most diabolical theories. Cincinnati
was shaken to its foundations and within an hour of the
announcement crowds were clamouring for tickets at the
court-house.

Fanny walked homewards with strangely mixed feelings.
On the one hand she hated any reminder of Nashoba: on the
other her generous mind acknowledged that if anybody
could rouse the town from its apathy Miss Wright, with her
rich, thrilling voice, her gift of oratory, her almost unpar-
alleled command of words, was the person to do it. No doubt
every word she spoke would lacerate the heart of one who had
so lately escaped from her spell, but it was imperative to hear
what she had to say and to watch the effect of her eloquence
upon the townsfolk.

As the day approached rumours flew round the city. The
crowds were going to be so great that the womenfolk would
be trampled underfoot. . . . A deputation of leading citizens
proposed to wait upon Miss Wright and forbid her to hold
the meeting on the grounds that it would cause disaffection
among the free Negroes . . . The lady was conveniently taken
ill and would not appear . . . It was said that the President
himself had issued instructions to boycott the affair. . . .

The lecture was timed for 7 p.m., but Fanny was bonneted
and cloaked by three and scurrying round the house exhort-
ing the family to hurry lest the throng stampede the hall
before they could reach it. Cecilia and Emily hastened to

obey, but there was a long wait for Henry and Hervieu who felt, not unnaturally, that if Miss Wright spied them she might spirit them back willy-nilly to her terrifying settlement. Even so the party arrived before the doors were open, which was a needless precaution because although the hall filled rapidly and every seat was occupied, there were no scenes of any kind.

Then Miss Wright walked on to the platform. . . . "It is impossible," wrote Fanny, "to imagine any thing more striking than her appearance. Her tall and majestic figure, the deep and almost solemn expression of her eyes, the simple contour of her finely formed head, unadorned, excepting by its own natural ringlets; her garment of plain white muslin, which hung around her in folds that recalled the drapery of a Grecian statue, all contributed to produce an effect, unlike anything I had ever seen before, or ever expect to see again."

The effect of this vision on Cincinnati was stupendous. Awed into silence, mouths agape, the audience swayed rhythmically to the notes of her deep, bell-like voice—and Fanny swayed too, even as she rated herself severely for behaving like a rabbit with a snake. Who knows but she might, without volition, have taken the next boat back to Memphis and Nashoba had not Frances Wright quoted Jefferson's favourite maxim, "All men are born free and equal."

As this phrase rolled forth she sat bolt upright, an expression of extreme disgust on her face. Through her study of American history she had conceived a hatred of Jefferson, whom she regarded as an "unprincipled tyrant and most heartless libertine." He had done deeds, she averred, which would make the sons of Europe shudder; he had fathered scores of children by his female slaves; he kept these miserable offspring in slavery too, his favourite cruelty being to make them serve him wine at his orgies; he roared with laughter when those white enough attempted to escape, saying, "Let the rogues get off, if they can; I will not hinder them!" Oh, there was no end to the sins of this adored leader of the democrats and to hear his "mischievous sophistry" so glibly quoted by one whose life was dedicated to the regeneration of the Negro race was too much altogether. For the rest of the evening Fanny's alert brain analysed every sentence of Miss Wright's speech, which was really only an introduction to the startling things she intended to say in later lectures. To her family's relief she made no attempt to join the admiring throng round the speaker and during the walk home she was unusually silent. Only on the doorstep did she say, "Nothing, absolutely nothing," in a firm voice; but she did not tell the children the words were a precise description of what the lecture would have signified if stripped of Grecian glamour and golden tongue.

A few weeks later she heard that a proposed second lecture from Miss Wright, at which a collection for Nashoba was to be made, had been abandoned owing to lack of support, and for the first time felt an affinity with the Cincinnatians. They too, apparently, had had the wit to discern the emptiness behind the façade. She had yet to learn that the only form of public meeting which held the power to move the citizens deeply and lastingly was a Revival.

Fanny had already been intrigued by the bewildering number of religious sects which flourished in the town and had caused considerable offence by remarking that if any stranger wishful of studying the latest feminine fashions visited Cincinnati he would do best to spend his time in the innumerable churches and chapels because only there were they displayed. She had also observed that the influence wielded by ministers over the female members of their congregations was comparable to the power of the priests over the women of Spain in an earlier age. But not until she had spent several months in the city did she realise exactly how the clergy managed to maintain their tenacious grip on their lady parishioners.

It was in early June that her acquaintances dropped their harmless gossip about each other's clothes and talked instead of the Revival. "The Revival will be very full." . . . "We shall be constantly engaged during the Revival." . . . "Mrs. S. is putting up the Rev. T." . . . "The Rev. C. is staying with the D's." . . .

By dint of tactful questioning Fanny discovered exactly what the Revival was. It appeared that the "un-national church of America needed to be roused, at regular intervals, to greater energy and exertion," and that twice a year clergymen of an immense variety of Presbyterian, Baptist and Methodist denominations toured the country, staying for a week or fortnight in smaller places, or for a month in larger centres such as Cincinnati. During their sojourn they held services twice daily and in addition presided over private meetings in the houses of those privileged to give them hospitality.

Fanny never received an invitation to a private meeting, but that did not prevent her from gathering the exciting information that the itinerant preacher greeted the guests as brothers and sisters, that everyone wore their best garments and partook of the choicest refreshments, and that after the social part of the evening the clergyman called upon those present to confess publicly all their thoughts, faults, and follies.

"These confessions are strange scenes," ruminated Fanny. "The more they confess, the more invariably are they encouraged and caressed. When this is over, they all kneel, and the Itinerant prays extempore. They then eat and drink again; and then they sing hymns, pray, exhort, sing and pray again, till the excitement reaches a very high pitch indeed."

At the principal Presbyterian church, however, she was twice an eye-witness of scenes which made her shudder. Several Itinerants took part in each service and after hymns and prayers one of them preached a fearful sermon about the decay of the human body after death. Then "he bent forward his head, as if to gaze on some object beneath the pulpit. And as Rebecca made known to Ivanhoe what she saw through the window, so the preacher made known to us what he saw in the pit that seemed to open before him. . . . No image that fire, flame, brimstone, molten lead, or red-hot pincers could supply, with flesh, nerves, and sinews quivering under them, was omitted. The perspiration ran in streams from the face of the preacher; his eyes rolled, his lips were covered with foam, and every feature had the deep expression of horror it would have borne, had he, in truth, been gazing at the scene he described."

Overcome by emotion the preacher retired, to be succeeded by a colleague who asked in a coaxing voice how many of the congregation wanted to avoid the hell their dear brother had made them see. Flinging wide his arms he besought the repentant to come forward to sit on the bench for anxious sinners. "Come then!" he cried. "Come to the anxious bench, and we will show you Jesus!"

During the singing of another hymn Fanny saw numbers of young women stumbling from the crowded pews and tottering up the aisles to the anxious bench. The clergymen bent down and whispered to them, whereupon the wretched creatures groaned, screamed, and fell writhing on the floor, calling on Jesus to help them. "More than once," wrote

Fanny severely, "I saw a young neck encircled by a reverend arm." The Itinerants then proclaimed the "tidings of salvation" to the congregation, who barked "Amen!" "Glory!" "Amen!" in reply, while the still prostrate penitents relapsed into hysterics or convulsions.

By the time the Itinerants moved on to the next town there was very little Fanny did not know about Revivals and in her usual outspoken fashion she gave her opinion of them in no measured terms:

> It is thus the ladies of Cincinnati amuse themselves; to attend theatres is forbidden; to play cards is unlawful; but they work hard in their families and must have some relaxation. For myself, I confess that I think the coarsest comedy ever written would be a less detestable exhibition for the eyes of youth and innocence than such a scene.

(*iv*)

But there was a brighter side to Cincinnati life. For some reason or another a Mr. Bullock, former proprietor of the Egyptian Hall in London, had bought a large estate on the Kentucky bank of the Ohio about two miles downriver and he and his charming wife devoted their time to beautifying their extensive grounds and noble mansion. To this couple the Trollopes brought an introduction from a mutual friend and Fanny's happiest hours were spent in visiting them. In their lovely lofty rooms filled with priceless paintings, china and glass, or in the exquisitely planned gardens that commanded a view of one of the Ohio's finest reaches she could forget all the trials and tribulations of her new life, enjoy once again the conversation she missed so much; while for their part Mr. and Mrs. Bullock were delighted to meet such an intelligent and witty companion who talked so animatedly of the world they knew, and who carried her burdens so gallantly. Immensely hospitable the Bullocks insisted upon the whole family spending as much time as possible with them; they also took the greatest interest in Fanny's ideas for Henry and in the paintings of Auguste Hervieu.

Then there was Mr. Flint, editor of the *Western Monthly Review* and author of several admirably written books, whom Fanny described as "the most agreeable acquantance I made in Cincinnati, and indeed one of the most talented men I ever met." His sense of satire (sometimes of sarcasm) greatly appealed to her; he was a brilliant conversationalist; his mind was rapier-sharp. Since he was American to the backbone and an ardent patriot he and Fanny indulged in violent verbal battles which exhilarated them both and they derived much enjoyment from poking fun at the few local intelligentsia, an occupation neither of them was able to resist.

Their favourite butt was a man known to his admirers as "the *serious* gentleman," who fancied his reputation as a scholar. Not surprisingly he detested Fanny and addressed her as Paul did the offending Jews—"he did not, indeed, shake his raiment at me, but he used his pocket-handkerchief so as to answer the purpose." Having heard him speak of Prior as a childish writer and of Chaucer and Spenser as authors who wrote in an unintelligible tongue, Fanny took an impish delight in laying traps for his unwary mind. She egged him on to talk of Byron, proved adroitly that he had only read those passages which the true lover of poetry wished he had never written. Then she murmured in her sweetest voice that she had never listened to any *serious* gentleman discussing Lord Byron at full length before. She dangled Pope before his nose and when he said, "He is so entirely gone by, that in *our* country it is considered quite fustian to speak of him," she gently replied that surely "The

Rape of the Lock" showed a little talent. At this the victim grew so agitated that Mr. Flint and Fanny thought him about to have an apoplectic seizure, but finally he muttered, with a quick shake of the handkerchief, "The very title. . . !"

Next she twitted him with Dryden.

"We only know Dryden by quotations, madam, and these, indeed, are found only in books that have long since had their day."

"And Shakespeare, sir?"

"Shakespeare, madam, is obscene, and, thank God, WE are sufficiently advanced to have found it out! If we must have the abomination of stage plays, let them at least be marked by the refinement of the age in which we live."

"This," said Fanny in an audible aside to Mr. Flint, "is certainly being *au courant du jour.*"

These little interludes were highly diverting but they were scarcely calculated to help Fanny in her plans for the conquest of Cincinnati. The serious gentleman's adorers included the wives and daughters of the most influential men in the district and the majority had gone out of their way to show small kindnesses to the Trollopes on their arrival. They had thought her a nice "old woman" but they could not forgive her unholy alliance with the caustic-tongued Mr. Flint, her sharp quips, her use of incomprehensible French phrases, above all her treatment of their idol. It just showed, they said, that you could never trust the English—and look at the dreadful remarks she made about hogs, drains, Mr. Dorfeuille's exhibition, President Jefferson, the Revival! If a woman spoke so indelicately in public her private thoughts simply did not bear thinking about.

Fanny went serenely on her way, little recking that her small indiscretions were shortly to come back at her with the force of a boomerang. Heartily sick of ordinary Cincinnati society she made friends with several people frowned upon for various reasons. There was Mr. Longworth, an expert who had introduced vine-growing to the western states (a blow to the whisky trade) and carried out successful experiments on an estate where he employed emigrant German labourers at less than a shilling a day and their food. There were the Price family, consisting of a jovial general practitioner who openly confessed he was an atheist, his placid chapel-going wife (greatly pitied by her neighbours), and two gay, pretty daughters who scandalised everybody by getting up private theatricals. Worst of all there was Hiram Powers, afterwards a sculptor famous for his statue, "The Greek Slave," but then an ingenuous youth of eighteen who acted as general factotum to Mr. Dorfeuille. Fanny marked him down at once and suggested they should design a representation of one of Dante's *bolgias* as described in the *Inferno*. His nimble fingers made the figures and designed the *décor;* her fertile brain supplied details of the poet's conceptions and concocted a long programme (vastly expensive) which gave translated quotations and told, in a fantastic variety of type-faces, all the horrors portrayed in the tableaux. Their enthusiasm outran their sense of caution and poor Mr. Dorfeuille wrung his hands as costs mounted, but Fanny assured him that during the following winter he would not only recoup his losses but reap far greater benefit than he had done from his Chamber of Horrors. She had good ideas too, she added darkly, about a yet more startling use of his electrical machine.

Having got the *bolgia* preparations well under way she felt free to devote her mind to the perfection of a wildly ambitious scheme which was to provide a career for Henry and a fortune for them all. She had heard from Thomas Anthony that he proposed joining them that summer and she wished to have every detail clear-cut before his arrival. Despite her experience of previous failures to arouse the artistic or intellectual sensibilities of the Cincinnatians she remained firm in the belief that they only required a lead and presto! away they would go on a positive orgy of culture. Whether the Bullocks, the Prices, Mr. Flint or Hiram Powers contributed to the idea or whether it was entirely her own is not known, but Fanny had determined to build and open in the city an establishment which would so inspire the inhabitants that they would crowd its portals the day and evening long.

According to Thomas Adolphus his mother visualised an "institution which, so far as I was able to understand the plan, was to combine the specialities of an Athenaeum, a lecture hall, and a bazaar!" There would be exhibitions of Hervieu's pictures and of Hiram Powers' sculptures; informative talks by erudite professors from the more civilised eastern states; amateur dramatic performances and visits from famous actors and musicians of different nationalities; balls, receptions and soirées of all descriptions. To pay for these delights (for Fanny insisted she had no illusions as to the speed of Cincinnati's reaction to culture) her thrifty brain had designed the bazaar part of the scheme. She knew full well the fondness of the local ladies for fashionable garments, trinkets, ornamental trifles for the home; and the impossibility of achieving such things in a shopless city. Her project simply could not fail to be successful.

To expostulations from Henry and Hervieu she turned a deaf ear. She was utterly repelled by the notion of starting in a small way. Hadn't they realised by now that Americans liked everything on the grand scale? She refused to tolerate any suggestion that dear Papa would not like her plan. Didn't he always applaud her common sense? As to asking the advice of some ignorant, tobacco-chewing lawyer—no, no, she would not hear of such a thing!

The boys gave up protest and Fanny's grandiose planning continued unchecked. Soon she had everything worked out to her satisfaction and even had her eye on a suitably central site. True, she did not actually negotiate for it, but the dragon's teeth were sown and Thomas Anthony's arrival would be the signal for them to spring, fully armed, from the ground.

There was another matter, however, that was yet more urgent—the renting of a better house. Their present quarters had never been comfortable and with the coming of the warm weather the Trollope nostrils were assailed by the frightful smells emanating from the deposits of black slime, the piles of refuse in the streets, and the omnipresent pigs. Thoroughly alarmed lest the family succumb to some dire complaint Fanny began a vigorous house-hunt and after a few weeks was fortunate enough to find a roomy, wood-built cottage in the little village of Mohawk, a mile and a half outside the city. Painted white, it had large airy rooms, an ice-house which never failed on the hottest day, a charming piazza looking across a grassy meadow to the fringes of the forest, and a well-stocked vegetable garden. For some reason the place was free of mosquitoes—and to Fanny's joy it possessed that Cincinnati rarity, green Venetian blinds!

She wisely lost no time in striking a bargain with the lawyer who owned it and was on the point of moving in when poor Henry developed a soaring temperature accompanied by the most distressing bilious symptoms. For a few days he was desperately ill, and though his mother had a high opinion of genial Dr. Price's capabilities she was shocked by his drastic treatment of the case. He resorted to repeated and violent bleeding and prescribed enormous quantities of calomel, that drug she already had good reason to fear. However, Henry's fever subsided. Gaunt as a scarecrow he was moved out to Mohawk, but it was many weeks before he could do more than crawl across the meadow.

Still he, no less than the others, appreciated country life. It was pleasant to gather fresh tomatoes from the garden, to spend the brilliant summer days sprawled full length under the forest trees with a book, to dream away the evenings on the piazza watching the splendid starry sky. Busy as she was with her hundred and one tasks and prospects Fanny too enjoyed the rustic scene. "We lived," she said, "on terms of primeval intimacy with our cow, for if we lay down on our lawn she did not scruple to take a sniff at the book we were reading, but then she gave us her own sweet breath in return." She also gave them pure fresh milk, a very real boon and as it was possible to buy butter, eggs and poultry from small farms near by there was no need to trudge into Cincinnati market.

But as usual Fanny's energy craved outlet—"mooning" was always frowned upon in her household. It was ridiculous to live on the very verge of the forest (a course of Mr. Fenimore Cooper's novels had smothered the forest fears born at Nashoba). Armed with parasols, drawing albums, sandwiches and books, she led her little flock into the trees and up a hill so steep that they "fancied we could rest ourselves against it by only leaning forward a little." At last they stood panting on the summit, only to find the trees so dense they had difficulty in drawing breath. On they stumbled knee-deep through "aboriginal leaves" seeking some less air-tight spot but soon all sank, exhausted, on to a fallen tree-trunk which being rotten, promptly gave way beneath their combined weight and deposited them in a mass of rotten rubbish already occupied by a great variety of angry insects. The

Trollopes were bitten, stung, scratched beyond endurance; their clothes were saturated with evil-smelling mud. Having extricated themselves with difficulty they were attacked by such droves of mosquitoes that they blundered blindly in what they imagined was the direction of home; but the trees were so thick, the descent on the carpet of dried leaves so slithery, that they quickly lost their bearings and paused to search for the sort of trail along which Mr. Cooper's wood-land characters always travelled. They failed to find one, but suddenly Fanny pointed ahead. There, she was convinced, was the moss-covered tree-stump they had passed on the way up. With glad cries she urged the party down a yet steeper slope and, sure enough, they soon reached the edge of the forest. Unfortunately it was not the right edge. In their confusion they had come down on the far side of the ridge and had to tramp three miles on a "corduroy" road under a blazing sun before they glimpsed their home. When they had partially recovered from their ordeal Henry, Cecilia and Emily forgot the rules of obedience drilled into their infant minds by their Papa and said with one voice that Mama must give them her faithful promise never, never again to propose a forest picnic. In the ordinary way this unwonted display of temerity would have been dealt with in summary fashion; but Fanny was in such a state of physical and nervous discomfort (who knew what fresh plagues the convalescent Henry might not have collected?) that she vowed in trembling tones there would be no more of these expeditions.

(*v*)

Outwardly, the rest of the summer passed peacefully, the only excitement being the Fourth of July celebrations at which Fanny rejoiced to note the gaiety and high spirits of

the townsfolk, though she could not refrain from the ce
sorious remark that "would they but refrain from spittir
on that hallowed day, I should say, that on the 4th of Jul
at least, they [the Americans] appeared to be an amiab
people." But as the thunderstorms for which the district wa
renowned crashed and rumbled overhead, so a faint ech
of that god-like anger sounded from the throats of th
family's Cincinnati acquaintances. "The English ol
woman," "that Mrs. Trollope with the foreign ways" wa
clearly up to no good. She had inveigled poor Mr. Dorfeuill
into spending his hard-earned money on the construction c
an immoral exhibition; she was downright rude to th
Mohawk farmers' wives who practised the usual welcomin
custom of walking uninvited into a newcomer's house for
friendly gossip; she had told one neighbour he would b
better advised to mend his fences than spend his time read
ing the political news in the local liquor store; she had de
nied the irrefutable fact that King George IV of Englan
snatched the few dollars any of his thrifty subjects manage
to save up; she had created a proper commotion about th
new slaughter-house for hogs that was building in the fiel
next to her meadow. . . .

Fanny was unaware of these mutterings. Summer wa
drifting toward autumn; yet Thomas Anthony had not pu
in an appearance and she was much exercised lest some un
foreseen circumstance had caused the postponement of hi
visit. After the manner of Bluebeard's wife she posted eithe
Cecilia or Emily at an upper window commanding the view
of the road leading from Cincinnati, calling from downstair
at intervals, "Sister Anne, Sister Anne, is there anybod
coming?" and she had almost given up hope of seeing he
husband until the spring when late one night he arrived

ringing a wonderful surprise—the beloved eldest son, Thomas Adolphus.

The boy had left Winchester in the July and as it was not et certain whether he would succeed to a scholarship of New College in several months' time his father had decided the oyage would be an excellent experience for him. But there vas, of course, the ever-present problem of finance and, more-ver, as there was a Spartan side to Thomas Anthony's char-cter which refused to allow him to spend money on personal omfort, they sailed for New York at the beginning of Sep-ember in the steerage of the ship *Corinthian*. Even Thomas Adolphus, whose enthusiasm for travel was such that he vould have crossed the Atlantic on a raft if necessary, found he passage tough; the sufferings of his delicate, morose fa-her must have been indescribable. The twenty or so steerage erths had absolutely no privacy, the ventilation was abom-nable, the quarters were revoltingly dirty, the other voyagers vere rather less than human. Thomas Anthony retired to his erth with one of his worst sick headaches before the ship ailed, and for thirty-eight interminable days he lay there hile his fellow-passengers fought, drank, cooked, swore, roaned and snored all around him. When he tottered ashore) be greeted by a Mr. Wilkes (the uncle or great-uncle of the elebrated Commodore Wilkes of the *Trent*), a former friend f the Reverend William Milton, he felt so ill that he might ave turned his face to the wall and died there and then had : not been for Mr. Wilkes's vehement disapproval of Miss rances Wright and all her works. Mails were so slow and nsure that several of Fanny's letters had not reached her usband. Little wonder, therefore, that he was extremely onfused as to what was actually happening and that the ere thought of her and the children being involved in some dangerous enterprise was sufficient to determine him to press on regardless of health.

Mr. Wilkes was most kind and arranged their coach journey to Cincinnati, but this proved almost as full of hardship as the ocean crossing. The route lay by Pittsburgh and the Allegheny Mountains, the "corduroy" roads were vile, the drivers took appalling risks and thought nothing of shaking every bone in their passengers' bodies, the nightly lodgings were rough and infested with bugs. Only the food was good —and food was the last thing to appeal to poor Thomas Anthony, who was prostrate from nervous exhaustion by the time he reached Mohawk.

But it was so wonderful to be reunited with his family and to find they had escaped Miss Wright's clutches that within a week he was feeling much better. His dear, capable Fanny cossetted him, made him dainty little invalid dishes, soothed away his headache with cold cloths and massage. She was so cheerful too (it was nearly a year since he had listened to her quick bright voice, heard her spontaneous peals of laughter) and the children had grown taller, more self-reliant. . . Thomas Anthony lay back against comfortably plumped-up pillows and thought for the first time in a long, long while that life was good.

It was at this propitious moment that Fanny unfolded the details of her brilliant scheme. She had been prepared for arguments, disapproval, querulous protests, and had carefully rehearsed answers to these; but her husband's appearance on arrival had so shocked her, so forcefully brought home the fact that he was an extremely sick man, that now she told him her plans quietly, without emphasis or eloquence. Never perhaps, had he been in more receptive mood. With his brain still dulled by recent sufferings he felt relaxed, at peace, only too grateful to let Fanny map out their future

nd what a fund of common sense she possessed! Why, she
ad thought of everything from a suitable site to the goods
ey should stock in the bazaar, from the cost of buildings to
e names of famous lecturers. Naturally, he was more inter-
ted in the cultural side of the establishment (though he
lmired the attention she paid to the commercial one) and
e thought the project excellent. Cincinnati was a new,
ourishing city of upwards of twenty thousand inhabitants,
l of whom were debarred, by the remoteness of their situa-
on, from enjoyment of the amenities of civilisation. Now
is clever Fanny proposed bringing these things to their very
oorstep and unconsciously he echoed her words, "It cannot
il."

To say that Fanny was relieved would be an understate-
ent. She knew far better than Thomas Anthony the thin-
ess of the financial tightrope on which they balanced, knew
o the necessity for instant action. The fact that the whole
anslation of the plan into reality would be her sole responsi-
ility exhilarated her and she plunged straightaway into
usiness negotiations. Within a week she had rented the plot
f land in the centre of the city, interviewed a builder, ex-
lained her ideas on design to an architect and found a
wyer with whom her husband could discuss legal matters.
hese preliminaries settled, her activities came to an abrupt
op as there was no hope of building being begun before the
oring, and while she bit her lip at Thomas Anthony's re-
eration of the Latin tag *"Festina lente"* she hid her vexa-
on and concentrated on the arranging of amusements for
e visitors.

Unlike Fanny both Thomas Anthony and Thomas Adol-
hus had visualised Cincinnati as a rough settlement in the
ackwoods. Consequently they were agreeably surprised by
verybody they met, everything they saw. Dr. Price and Mr.

Flint were men after the disputatious Thomas Anthony
own heart, for they argued as fiercely as he did and took n
umbrage when he laid down the law, while instead of recoi
ing before the social habits of the townsfolk he studied ther
with the ardour displayed by an anthropologist studying th
aborigines. Thomas Adolphus, normally a shy youth, wa
quite captivated by the sparkling Price girls and, though h
strenuously refused to dance at their frequent parties, wa
persuaded to act the part of Falstaff in their performance c
The Merry Wives of Windsor. He also made great friend
with Mr. Longworth, from whom he learnt much about vit
culture, and he spent a lot of time assisting the adventurou
Hiram Powers in the execution of the *bolgia* tableaux.

Visits to the Bullocks' estate and long rambles through th
countryside made them anxious to explore further; so it wa
arranged that they should go, with Henry and Hervieu, t
two unusual places, the first bearing the extraordinary nam
of Big-Bone Lick. This lay on the Kentucky side of the Ohi
and consisted of a huge bed of blue clay in which reposed th
mammoth bones of long extinct mammals and reptiles. Th
clay was so slippery and treacherous that Thomas Anthon
contented himself with the role of onlooker, but the thre
young men dug in the gluey mass with such energy that the
unearthed several enormous bones which they bore home i
triumph.

Their second expedition was to Mount Lebanon, som
twenty-five miles from Cincinnati, and the home of a sec
known as the Shaking Quakers. These people had bough
land when it was of little value and by their efforts had estab
lished a prosperous farming settlement where an equa
number of men and women lived in amity. Their laws pro
hibited any cohabitation and no people with children wer
accepted as members, with the result that the community wa

ntirely childless. Both sexes worked very hard, not only on
the land but in the manufacture of various articles useful in
country life, and they ran a simple hostel where outsiders
could stay at moderate cost. Solemn, taciturn, they seemed
to derive little pleasure from life despite the fact that they
had amassed considerable wealth, and at stated intervals they
held religious ceremonies at which they jumped and shook
themselves like dervishes. They appeared exceedingly healthy
but reminded the visitors of a herd of well-kept animals
rather than a collection of human beings.

Cecilia and Emily were deeply impressed by tales of the
shaking Quakers, begging their mother that they too might
pay a visit to the community. This Fanny refused to consider,
saying acidly they had already witnessed equally deplorable
scenes at Revival meetings, a remark which led Thomas Anthony (who had not attended one) to remonstrate with her
length. But apart from this little brush the family passed
peaceful, happy winter marred only by thought of the
father's and eldest son's near departure.

Through the long evenings Fanny and Thomas Anthony
discussed every detail of their future. On his return to England he would see Thomas Adolphus settled in at New College (for of course the coveted fellowship would materialise),
invest their small remaining capital in stock for the bazaar
(this to be shipped direct to America), sublet both farms at an
advantageous rental, sell up the furniture, arrange for Anthony to board with relatives during the Harrow vacations,
and himself sail back across the Atlantic for the grand opening of the wonderful establishment which was to keep the
entire family in affluence for evermore. Meanwhile Fanny
would remain at Mohawk with Henry and the girls to supervise building operations, compose attractive advertisements,

engage artistes, lecturers and assistants, and settle the cour
less small problems bound to arise.

It may seem strange that Thomas Anthony, who apa
from his disputatiousness had been a good Chancery ba
rister, saw no blemish on the rosy picture conjured up 1
study of all these plans. But although Fanny's ministratio
and the quiet life he led at Mohawk had resulted in a te
porary respite from headaches his general health was rapid
deteriorating, his susceptibilities were somewhat dulled. 1
was therefore content to believe what he wished to belie
and when the *bolgia* exhibition turned out a roaring succe
(due in certain measure to some blood-curdling verses 1
Fanny, which were pasted up on doors and walls and whie
described the fearful doom that awaited any mortal foolhar
enough to touch the metal rod—electrically charged by Hira
Powers) he really felt that at long last fortune was turning
favourable eye on Trollopian endeavour. He even yielded
his wife's plea that he should travel home in comfort ar
acquiesced meekly when she declared he and Thomas Add
phus *must* visit the Great Lakes and Niagara before leavir
America.

By the beginning of February 1829 all was ready for the
departure. Worried lest father and son should succumb
the icy weather they might encounter on the overland part
their journey, Fanny bought two enormous buffalo-hide rob
and insisted they have double-soled shoes made. Obedien
but acutely conscious of their shaggy appearance, the pa
were about to embark on a steam-boat for Pittsburgh whe
news flashed through the town that General Jackson, tl
newly elected President, was expected to arrive at any momen
Since he too was going to Pittsburgh by ordinary boat—Fan
noted sternly that the "decent dignity of a private conve
ance" was not deemed necessary for him—she immediate

decided that such a golden opportunity of voyaging with the great was not to be missed. The passages were cancelled and Thomas Anthony and his first-born donned and took off their buffalo-robes several times before rumor gave way to fact and, to the accompaniment of the boom of cannon, the President's steam-boat, flanked by two others, swept up to the landing-stage.

Fanny was highly indignant at the behaviour of the huge crowd gathered to welcome General Jackson. Not a single huzza was raised and the people fell back in silence as he walked to the hotel. She was pleased, however, when her men folk were introduced to him, and relieved when Thomas Anthony managed to secure two berths. The excitement served to dull the pain of parting, but when she afterwards received a letter from her husband describing most interesting conversations held with the President, who had lately lost a dearly loved wife, and deploring the "brutal familiarity" with which he was treated at every stopping-place she again waxed wrathful over American manners.

"There was not," wrote Thomas Anthony, " a hulking boy from a keel-boat who was not introduced to the President, unless, indeed, as was the case with some, they introduced themselves: for instance, I was at his elbow when a greasy fellow accosted him thus:

" 'General Jackson, I guess?'

"The General bowed assent.

" 'Why, they told me you was dead.'

" 'No! Providence has hitherto preserved my life.'

" 'And is your wife alive too?'

"The General, apparently much hurt, signified the contrary, upon which the courtier concluded his harangue, by saying, 'Aye, I thought it was the one or the t'other of ye.' "

"Enthusiasm," commented Fanny dryly, "is not either the virtue or the vice of America."

From subsequent letters she was thankful to learn that they had encountered no gales or snowstorms while crossing the mountains, that they had much enjoyed their tour of the lakes, that they preferred Trenton Falls to mighty Niagara and that the kind offices of Mr. Wilkes had secured them two comfortable berths in a ship bound for England.

Perhaps it was as well Thomas Anthony forebore to mention that travel had brought on a succession of terrible headaches, or that Mr. Wilkes had condemned the Cincinnati project even more forcibly than he had the Nashoba one, for no sooner had the rest of the family waved farewell to their dear ones than clouds began to mass on the horizon.

(*vi*)

First Auguste Hervieu resigned his post at the drawing school. From the beginning he had found it difficult to maintain discipline in his large mixed class of boys and girls and had remonstrated in vain with his German employer about the way in which the pupils chattered, laughed and wandered around the room while he was instructing them. As the class grew more unruly so Hervieu became more annoyed, and one day he printed a set of rules on a large sheet of paper and pinned it to the school door. The German promptly removed the rules, gabbling, "Very goot, very goot in Europe, but America boys and girls will not bear it, dey vill do just vat dey please; Suur, dey vould go all avay next day!"

"And you will not enforce these regulations *si nécessaires*, Monsieur?" queried Hervieu stiffly.

His employer gave a vigorous shake of the head. "O, lar! not for de vorld!"

"*Eh bien,* monsieur," bowed the younger man, "I must leave the young republicans to your management."

Naturally the Trollopes applauded their friend's temerity; but the dismal fact remained that by his action he had not only lost five hundred dollars a year but antagonised the wealthy parents of Cincinnati to such an extent that it was exceedingly unlikely he would find any other work. A cross and worried Fanny did nothing to improve his chances by making audible and derogatory remarks about the appalling ignorance of the citizens on artistic matters, declaring that a rich man who viewed Mr. Bullock's collection of engravings had drawled, "Have you really done all these since you came here? How hard you must have worked!" and that a second gentleman renowned for his taste had, on being shown a drawing of Hebe and the bird sacred to Jupiter, demanded to know the female's name. On being told it was Hebe he had sneered, "Hebe? What the devil has Hebe to do with the American eagle?"

Then there were endless obstacles in the way of building the great Athenaeum-bazaar. The contractors muttered about the wet spring; the architect regretted he could not follow Mrs. Trollope's designs; the professors, actors and musicians that were written to either failed to reply or sent a brief refusal of the proposed engagement; and not a young man or woman in Cincinnati evinced the slightest desire to enrol as an assistant. Day after day Fanny marched into the city to chivvy apathetic workmen and stand fuming in front of the gaunt, half-finished walls which never seemed a single inch higher.

There was a sad falling-off too in the attendance figures for the *bolgia* exhibition and, much to the dismay of Fanny and

Hiram Powers, Mr. Dorfeuille point-blank refused to consider the production of further tableaux. Enough, he said in effect, was as good as a feast and he had no intention of wasting the profits he had netted the previous winter. He might have added, had he so chosen, that Mrs. Trollope's growing reputation as Cincinnati's most severe, most unfair critic, was such that anything sponsored by her was bound to fail. And there is little doubt that this was the case.

It was all very unfortunate. There was no real malice in Fanny. She had the kindest heart imaginable, but she simply could not resist saying what she thought—and the thoughts were thoroughly unpopular. Cincinnati resented the way her quick, darting mind pounced on their shortcomings, shook them, held them up to the light for all to see. People were truly hurt by her rapier-sharp tongue (and one can sympathise with them) because it ridiculed and derided many things dear to them, from Revivals to hogs, and they felt also that she had ill-rewarded the hospitality shown to a stranger. Since they could not fight her with her own weapons they decided, quietly and firmly, to have nothing more to do with any of her mad schemes. In short, they beat a strategic retreat, leaving her in splendid isolation at Mohawk.

Not that Fanny so much as noticed their withdrawal—to begin with. The little time she could spare from harrying builders, carpenters and decorators was spent in visiting the Bullocks, arguing with Mr. Flint, discussing viticulture with Mr. Longworth or encouraging the Price girls to get up more amateurish theatricals. But in early summer she accompanied the Bullocks to a huge camp-meeting in the backwoods of Indiana, found to her horror that it was a Revival on the grand scale, and on her return attended a city function at which she described the "atrocious wickedness" of the scene and quoted Milton's words:

Blind mouths! that scarce themselves know how to hold
A sheep-hook, or have learned aught else the least
That to the faithful herdsman's art belongs! . . .
And when they list, their lean and flashy songs,
Grate on their scrannel pipes of wretched straw;
The hungry sheep look up, and are not fed,
But swoln with wind, and the rank mist they draw,
Rot inwardly—and foul contagion spread.

The Cincinnatians were not so bone-headed as she imagined them. As they listened to her violent denunciation of one of their most cherished ceremonies their faces froze into expressionless masks. The change was immediately apparent to the observant Fanny. Genuinely distressed at having given offence she began to talk at length on some innocuous subject; but the harm was done and by the end of the evening it was all too clear that no effort of hers could undo it.

It was now borne in upon Fanny that the very people she hoped to educate and entertain through her Athenaeum-bazaar harboured the darkest thoughts about her. Had she been in her usual brisk health she would probably have thrust this unwelcome knowledge from her and used every ounce of her undoubted charm to wheedle the Americans back to their earlier friendliness; but for a week or two she had been conscious of a general malaise and within twenty-four hours of her outburst over the camp-meeting she was laid low with fever.

Like most energetic folk she was an extraordinarily bad patient. Cecilia and the French cook were driven almost distracted by her orders, counter-orders and insistence that this, that or the other duty be performed without delay. Henry and Hervieu toiled to and from Cincinnati in the heat several times a day—fruitless journeys since the workmen merely smiled, shrugged their shoulders and turned away when asked urgent questions. Dr. Price cajoled, bullied, dosed and bled his recalcitrant patient, but said privately to the children that he was very worried about her condition. Her temperature remained high, the pains in her limbs acute, and she seemed bereft of any rallying power, a fact which sorely puzzled the doctor, for apathy was the last quality he expected from his vivacious, quick-minded friend.

For many years Fanny had consistently over-taxed her body, so it was not surprising that she was in no physical state to resist the particularly virulent brand of malaria that had attacked her; but Dr. Price might have been even more disturbed had he known that the aches in his patient's limbs were as nothing beside the agonising thoughts which crowded her brain. With a sudden, awful clarity of vision she saw the grand building for which she had planned so strenuously reach completion only to collapse like a house of cards because of the relentless enmity—yes, yes, there was no other word—of these dull, brutal backwoodsmen who had no more sensitivity than the pigs surrounding them. And when tragedy occurred what would happen to the children and Thomas Anthony? There would be no capital left, not even enough to pay homeward passages. She, Henry, Cecilia and Emily would be doomed to live out their lives in this hateful land that breathed fever and death. Fanny lay rigid, with closed eyes, brooding over this ghastly future, imagining herself and the girls as hired "Helps," Henry as a tender of hogs, while across the ocean Thomas Anthony struggled with headaches, farms, and the education of Thomas Adolphus and Anthony.

Dr. Price had resorted to large doses of calomel (that drug which seemed to haunt the Trollopes) before slowly, very slowly, Fanny began to recover. For weeks after her temperature was normal, however, she was so weak that she had to remain in bed. Her friend Mr. Flint sent quantities of books for her to read during convalescence. His own novel, *Frances*

Berrian, was a good choice, as were Miss Sedgewick's books, but since his admiration for Fanny was tempered by distress at her dislike of western America's forests he most unhappily included the entire works of Mr. Fenimore Cooper with an earnest plea that she should study them. She did, with dire results:

> By the time these American studies were completed, I never closed my eyes without seeing myriads of bloody scalps floating round me; long slender figures of Red Indians crept through my dreams with noiseless tread; panthers glared; forests blazed; and whichever way I fled, a light foot, a keen eye, and a long rifle were sure to be on my trail. An additional ounce of calomel hardly sufficed to neutralize the effect of these raw-head and bloody-bones adventures. I was advised to plunge immediately into a course of fashionable novels. It was a great relief to me; but as my head was by no means very clear, I sometimes jumbled strangely together the civilised rogues and assassins of Mr. Bulwer, and the wild men, women, and children slayers of Mr. Cooper; and, truly, between them, I passed my dreams in very bad company.

Fortunately she presently regained sufficient strength of will to discard these lively tales and re-read Scott's *Waverley Novels.* Under their magic her nightmares disappeared, she "ceased to be languid and fretful," and she was able to sit up in a chair for the greater part of each day, but "it was nine weeks before I left my room, and when I did, I looked more fit to walk into the Potter's Field (as they call the English burying-ground) than anywhere else."

Fanny was prone to exaggeration at times, but in this case she erred on the side of understatement, for many months were to pass before she was really well. During that time she had to endure such a succession of tribulations that, had she been a creature of lesser courage, she would surely have turned her face to the wall and died.

No sooner was she promoted to the taking of short airings in an open carriage than Henry was seized with a second, more violent attack of the mysterious bilious ailment he had suffered a year earlier. This culminated in fits of ague so awful to watch that Fanny wrote:

> I believe this frightful complaint is not immediately dangerous; but I never can believe that the violent and sudden prostration of strength, the dreadfully convulsive movements which distort the limbs, the livid hue that spreads itself over the complexion, can take place without shaking the seat of health and life. Repeatedly we thought the malady cured, and for a few days the poor sufferer believed himself restored to health and strength; but again and again it returned upon him, and he began to give himself up as the victim of ill health.

Despite her own weakness Fanny nursed him with her usual efficiency, refusing at first to believe the truth that was becoming all too evident—that Henry's malady was more ominous than fever or biliousness. Then, as though to mock her, the Cincinnati builders put on a sudden spurt and actually completed the structure of the Athenaeum-bazaar in the very same week that Dr. Price told her bluntly that there was no hope of Henry's ever being strong enough to run such a place or even help in it. He went further; he said that no matter how carefully the boy was tended he would not survive another twelve months in Cincinnati's climate.

For over a year Fanny had fiercely insisted to herself and everybody else that Henry's delicacy was caused by outgrowing his strength and would vanish as soon as adolescence was passed; yet in her heart she had feared that some day she would hear this dread pronouncement. Now it had come and, as sometimes happens, that secret fear seemed to add to, rather than detract from, the force of the blow. As she faced the compassionate gaze of the brusque little doctor despair swept her. Henry, dear gentle Henry, was dying and she was powerless to help him because she herself had come to the end of her strength, money, hope. Before that appalling knowledge all lesser anxieties were forgotten; her whole being was concentrated on Henry. Henry as a small boy, round face aglow, stammering out stories of coaches, ships, people seen on his London rambles; Henry asking endless questions as he trotted after her round the Harrow farm; Henry in his first long trousers; Henry laughing delightedly at sight of an American frame house being moved from one place to another by a team of forty oxen. . . .

Presently she became aware that Dr. Price was asking her if there was anything he could do. With a tremendous effort she said "no," thanked him for all his kindness, even accompanied him to his waiting buggy and waved him goodbye after sending affectionate messages to his wife and daughters. But as he drove back to the city memory of her agonised eyes, her frail erect figure, stayed with him. What an indomitable woman she was! And what tragedy lay ahead of her! for if he was not very much mistaken, little fair-haired Emily already showed signs of the consumption which ravaged her brother. Dr. Price scowled and flicked the air savagely with his whip. "Rachel sorrowing for her children," he muttered. Then he caught himself up with a jerk; an avowed agnostic had no right to think of Rachel.

(*vii*)

For the next few days Fanny pleaded indisposition and kept to her room, fearful lest word or look betray her grief. Hour after hour she sat by her window staring out unseeing at the blaze of autumn colourings, forcing her numbed mind to consideration of what must be done, and as her thoughts began to resolve more quickly so her native courage returned. Dr. Price had said another year of Cincinnati's climate would kill Henry—ah, but he need not remain another month, another week in this region of plague and pestilence! A certain sum of money had been set aside for living expenses and the furnishing and starting of the Athenaeum-bazaar. The thing to do, therefore, was to sell the newly finished building, sublet the Mohawk cottage and set out on the homeward journey to England forthwith, the only impediment to this brisk programme being that Thomas Anthony might have already left home to join them in America. The risk, however, had to be taken and a suddenly revitalised Fanny swept from her retreat, calling imperiously on Cecilia, Hervieu and Emily to assist in the necessary arrangements.

Almost sixty years later Thomas Adolphus wrote of his mother: "Her mind was one of the most extraordinarily constituted in regard to recuperative power and the capacity of throwing off sorrow, that I ever knew or read of. Any one who did not know her, as her own son knew her, might have supposed that she was deficient in sensibility. No judgment could have been more mistaken. She felt acutely, vehemently. But she seemed to throw off sorrow as, to use the vulgar phrase, a duck's back throws off water, because the nature of the organism will not suffer it to rest there." He was right. Fanny possessed the resilience of an indiarubber ball, but even her closest friends in Cincinnati (with the exception of the shrewd Dr. Price who kept his own counsel) were genuinely shocked by her seeming heartlessness, while those who cordially disliked her nudged each other at sight of the woefully emaciated Henry and whispered that the

"English old woman" was a monster determined on the destruction of her own child.

In truth Fanny was fighting for that child's life with a fervour which should have called forth admiration from her most bitter enemy, but in her usual fashion she seized upon Dr. Price's remark about climate and unfortunately told everyone she met that had they not been obliged to settle in the "mephitic airs" of the Ohio, Henry would never have known a day's illness. People sniffed—nor could one blame them. Henry was a walking bean-pole on arrival, the girls were pale little creatures; and far from being forced to live in Cincinnati, Mrs. Trollope not only voluntarily chose it as a dwelling-place but had spent the past eighteen months condemning the usages and customs of its citizens.

Fanny, dashing hither and thither on a multitude of urgent errands, was sublimely unconscious of what was being said. Her one aim was to leave the horrid place at the earliest possible moment and she had very nearly completed her preparations when fate dealt her a further series of stunning blows.

A lugubrious letter from Thomas Anthony informed her that despite the most valiant efforts he had failed to find a tenant for either farm, while Lord Northwick showed a distressing reluctance to discuss any possible break in the lease. Worse still, there was no hope of a vacancy at New College for Thomas Adolphus, and rather than waste the two exhibitions the boy had received from Winchester he had decided he should enter Alban Hall, of which college that famous Liberal, Dr. Whately (later Archbishop of Dublin) was Principal. Argumentative even in letters Thomas Anthony then gave details of why a university education was an absolute necessity, explained at length the severe privations he himself would have to undergo in order to keep his eldest son at

Oxford, and wound up with a dramatic account of the incessant headaches caused by all these worries. He added, almost casually, that Anthony was well and that a large consignment of goods for the bazaar had been despatched.

There was nothing Fanny would not have done to help husband or children, but as she finished the letter she wished wildly for a magic carpet that she might fly to Harrow and shake Thomas Anthony until his teeth rattled in his head. At that moment, however, Henry approached her with a letter he had received from his brother. In the letter Thomas Adolphus, who had never before ventured criticism of his parent, confessed that Papa's irascibility had increased to such a degree that he was impossible to live with. The long adopted policy of answering all his provocative questions with a gentle "Yes, sir," or "No, sir," did not satisfy him now. He *would* be argued with, and the argument always led to "scenes of painful violence, which I have reason to fear hasten the return of his suffering."

Fanny was aghast. Could her poor dear husband be going out of his mind? Perhaps owing to her recent study of Mr. Fenimore Cooper's works her mind held a ghastly vision of Thomas Anthony cleaving his sons' skulls with a hatchet. Oh, if they could only get home quickly, quickly, before some dire tragedy occurred! If she were on the spot she could cope with things, but at this distance. . . . In her agitation she flung on bonnet and cloak and set out to walk to Cincinnati. No matter what it cost her, she was going to book their passages on the next Pittsburgh-bound steam-boat.

The shipping clerks looked vacant, chewed quids of tobacco, spat out the noxious juice. No, there weren't any berths available, no hope of any for weeks to come; but would the "English old lady" care to take delivery of some mighty great packages which had arrived for her? These proved to contain the bazaar goods and for the next week Fanny watched in grim silence as the girls and Hervieu unpacked them. Whether Thomas Anthony had mislaid the long lists she had given him or whether he had thought his own choice best was not clear, but in a vast miscellaneous collection ranging from feathers and ribbons to lamps and pots and pans there was not a solitary article on which the ladies of Cincinnati would have bestowed more than a passing glance. Everything was of the shoddiest (though she could not bear to think of what the freight had cost), but the greatest irony of all, to her mind, was that the consignment had arrived after the entire project had been abandoned.

Life, thought Fanny, had become intolerable. If she stayed at home she sat surrounded by this gargantuan assortment of rubbish: if business took her into the city she saw, before ever she reached it, the imposing façade of the Athenaeum-bazaar towering against the skyline: if, as too often happened, she had to show prospective purchasers round its empty, echoing halls she was forced to listen to the cruellest criticism. Everybody reckoned it was plain foolish to have a building more than two stories high; they said it seemed a shame to waste all that money on a place fit neither for a slaughter-house for hogs nor a paper-mill, they just couldn't imagine what anyone had ever thought they could *do* with it. Fanny kept a polite smile on her lips, but every word fell like a drop of vitriol on her heart.

Then came the final and heaviest blow. As a rule Cincinnati enjoyed a long autumn before the wet weather set in, but this year autumn was cut short by a frost unprecedented in severity or length. First the Licking, and then the Ohio, froze. No steam-boats could run, the rough roads were impassable. Willy-nilly the Trollopes were immured in Cincinnati for the winter; and there was no news from Harrow, for no mails could get through.

Fanny's state of mind may be imagined. In front of her anxious eyes was Henry, doomed to die unless he could be removed to a more salubrious climate. Far across the Atlantic were Thomas Anthony, Thomas Adolphus and Anthony, living in heaven knew what state of enmity and misery. Worst of all, to one of her volatile temperament, there was no way in which she could alleviate distress, combat disaster. All through November she fumed and fretted. Every night when she went to bed she remarked hopefully that she was sure a thaw was setting in: every morning when she awakened she stared out at the snow-covered lawn, the bare forest trees that stood like sentinels in the icy windless air.

Such continued frustration was not to be borne. Fanny turned her back on wintry view and busied herself with the sale of the bazaar stock. By dint of some hard bargaining she obtained better prices than she had hoped for (though she was under no illusion as to the over-all loss) and stimulated by this mild success she renewed her efforts to get rid of the white elephant of a building in the town. Whether she managed to sell or let it is not clear, but she seems to have disposed of it in some manner and while it is extremely unlikely the deal was a satisfactory one in the financial sense, at least it relieved her of further responsibility.

But the frost showed no sign of abating; in fact, the weather prophets predicted it would last another three months. Fanny therefore cast about for some other ploy. Earlier in the year Captain Basil Hall, an English naval officer, had published a book entitled *Travels in North America* which had caused a terrific upset in the States. "It was a sort of moral earthquake," wrote Fanny, "and the vibration it occasioned through the nerves of the Republic, from one corner of the Union to the other, was by no means over when I left the country in July 1831, a couple of years after the shock." Every paper, from the *American Quarterly Review* to the smallest local publication had printed violent denunciations of Captain Hall's works. It was asserted there was no word of truth in the book, that its author was a coarse man of "equivocal morals," that he had rewarded American hospitality by libelling his hosts, and that the British government had commissioned him to write the book in order to stop the growing admiration of the British people for the American way of life!

Greatly to her annoyance Fanny had been unable to obtain a copy. Cincinnati did not possess a bookshop, and had it done, so the citizens assured her stoutly, it would not have sold such a monstrous book. Even Mr. Flint failed her and requests to booksellers in bigger cities merely brought evasive replies which increased her wrath because every traveler who came to Cincinnati by steam-boat or stage-coach had just read the book and was loud in condemnation of it.

Her sympathies were all with Captain Hall and from study of the reviews and cross-examination of those who had read his work she gleaned the information that he, with his wife and child, had arrived armed with introductions to every individual of note and had been received everywhere in "full drawing-room style." At the time she had wondered wryly what he would have written had he stayed in America under the conditions she and her family endured; now, in her December isolation, she remembered Captain Hall, remembered also the copious diaries she had kept ever since leaving England. Why shouldn't *she* write a book about America, setting down fully and faithfully all she had seen and heard during her two years in the country?

The more she thought over the idea the more it appealed to her. In order to show their detestation of his opinions the Americans had bought edition after edition of Captain Hall's book, which had sold remarkably well in Britain too. It was well worth while, thought Fanny, to incur the wrath of the States if it brought you a nice fat sum in dollars. Besides, how satisfying it would be to tell the *real truth* about a people and country at whose hands she and hers had suffered so much.

For the rest of the winter Fanny was prodigiously busy. Her ordinary tasks were manifold enough and she would have considered it wrong to neglect them; but by the time she had attended to the housekeeping, given Cecilia and Emily their lessons, set Henry and Hervieu to useful occupations and superintended the dressmaking operations on which the girls were always engaged, there were precious few hours left for writing. She tackled the problem, however, with a vigour and method which would cause many a modern author to quail. Long before the rest of the household was astir she rose, dressed and sat down at her desk. Stimulated by sips of green tea, her blue hands encased in mittens, she wrote steadily by the light of a tallow dip until breakfast-time. After the early evening meal she again retired to her room and wrote until midnight—or later if necessary, for a target of a certain number of words had to be reached each day. This rigorous regime would have tried a woman in the full tide of youthful strength; when one remembers that Frances Trollope was in her fiftieth year, was not yet fully recovered from her bout of fever, and was a tyro at authorship, one can only marvel at her powers of endurance.

Her timing was perfect. By the end of February, when the breaking-up of the ice on the Licking and Ohio rivers filled the air with stupendous crashes as ice floes collided in the swirling waters, she had written the story of her two years' experiences. What is more, she was so engrossed in her book that although she was still determined to leave Cincinnati as soon as possible, she had abandoned any notion of going straight home to England. If her *Domestic Manners of the Americans* was going to achieve a large sale it must include descriptions of life in many different parts of the country and it was necessary therefore that she should visit as many other States as she could. Thanks to the sale of the bazaar stock, the disposal of the building and her own thrift there was sufficient money (provided the greatest care was practised) for her and the children to do a protracted tour. Hervieu, now practically an adopted son, would pay his own expenses and accompany them as he was very anxious to illustrate the book.

Fanny's despair of a brief few months before seemed to have vanished with the winter snows; yet there had been no news from Harrow and for all she knew the situation there might have worsened. Resilient as ever she pushed thought of Harrow away and kept reminding herself and Dr. Price how much, *much* better dear Henry was looking and how mistaken (not to say cruel) medical diagnosis of his complaint had been. The doctor pointed out that the improvement in Henry's health was temporary, caused simply by the long spell of cold dry weather, and that the quickest way to bring about a relapse was to subject the boy to a long spell of travel involving swift climatic changes and inevitable discomfort. He might as well have talked to thin air. Fanny had her head; there was no holding her.

In the first week in March the Trollopes embarked in the steam-boat *Lady Franklin*. The younger members of the party leaned over the deck-rail pointing out familiar landmarks as the boat swung into midstream, but Fanny retired to the ladies' cabin for "we left nought to regret at Cincinnati. The only regret was, that we had ever entered it; for we had wasted health, time, and money there." Unfortunately she glanced out of the window at precisely the wrong moment and saw, silhouetted against the pale spring sky, the one building in the city she wished particularly to forget.

(*viii*)

For the next fifteen months Fanny pursued her investigations into the American character with relentless thoroughness. After a whirlwind tour of Wheeling, West Virginia, and an excruciatingly bumpy stage-coach journey over the Alleghenies they reached Baltimore, which she found a surprisingly handsome city full of elegantly dressed women. They then took another steam-boat through Chesapeake Bay and up the Potomac River to Washington where, greatly to the relief of her exhausted family, she announced they would remain for a month so that she might study the political scene. To her delight, she met a very old friend, an Englishwoman who was the widow of an American, and had a delightful house some ten miles from the city near Stonington, Maryland, close to the Falls of the Potomac. Nothing would satisfy this kind creature but that the party should spend the summer at her home. Fanny accepted immediately and while she dashed round the countryside asking a myriad of questions on all manner of subjects from slavery to copperhead snakes and electioneering, the girls, Henry and Hervieu were able to lead a deliciously idle existence.

In late August, however, Fanny decided on a strenuous fortnight in Philadelphia, a city which taught her much. On the insistence of her friend they returned to Stonington for a brief stay before resuming their journeyings, and for the

second year in succession Fanny "again felt the noxious influence of an American autumn" and succumbed to a bad
attack of fever. Distressing though this was for her, one feels
that a kindly providence was shielding Henry from the gruel-
ling winter itinerary mapped out by his indefatigable parent. Her health returned so slowly that she was forced to
abandon her plans and yield to the suggestion that she should
move to the healthily situated town of Alexandria, some
fifteen miles distant, where there was an exceedingly capable
doctor. Here, in cheap and pleasant lodgings, the family
spent another very severe winter; but this time Fanny proved
a remarkably quiescent patient through her long convalescence, for she spent all her time on her book.

By now, of course, several letters had been exchanged
between her and Thomas Anthony, who was gloomily resigned to her continued absence although, to her indignation,
he was convinced that the *Domestic Manners of the Americans* would be refused by every publisher in England. He
made the barest of references to the farms (a fact which
should have aroused suspicions in her bosom), gave melancholy details of his headaches, and wrote somewhat vaguely
that Thomas Adolphus was enjoying life at Alban Hall and
that Anthony was progressing in mediocre fashion at Harrow.
With her amazing faculty for believing what she wished to
believe Fanny assured herself that the ominous news of a year
earlier must have been grossly exaggerated. She was further
heartened by dutiful but non-committal letters from both
her sons.

In the early spring of 1831, she told the children, they
would visit New York, then travel to Niagara—unthinkable
that they should leave America without visiting that wonder
of nature—return to New York and sail for home about the
beginning of July. Meanwhile would Henry and Hervieu be

so good as to obtain some pieces of smoked glass, as she understood a solar eclipse was to occur on February 12th.

They were duly impressed by the eclipse, "nearer total than any I ever saw," wrote Fanny, "or ever shall see," and shortly afterwards they left for New York, finding the journey agreeable as far as Trenton, where they exchanged a comfortable steam-boat for the "most detestable stage-coach that ever Christian built to dislocate the joints of his fellowmen." About New York itself Fanny was so enthusiastic that she actually spent seven weeks in the city before undertaking the Niagara trip, and returned for another fortnight afterwards. Thanks to the amiable Mr. Wilkes she was able to visit theatres, exhibitions and museums, while his friends showered hospitality on her and the children.

But fascinating as she found New York, Fanny sighed with relief when the day of departure arrived and she walked up the ship's gangway with scarcely a glance at the glittering loveliness of the harbour, clutching under one arm the "six hundred pages of griffonage" she had written. "Isn't it wonderful, Mama, to be going at last?" asked the excited Emily.

"Yes," said Fanny a trifle absently, but she wasn't really thinking of Harrow, or Thomas Adolphus and Anthony, or even of Thomas Anthony. She was thinking of the fame and fortune she held tightly against her side and so soon as she reached the cabin she spread out her papers and began to write:

> I remember hearing it said, many years ago, when the advantages and disadvantages of a particular residence were being discussed, that it was the "who?" and not the "where?" that made the difference between the pleasant and the unpleasant residence. The truth of the observation has been recalled to my mind since, by the constantly recurring evidence of its justness. In applying this to America, I speak not of my friends, nor of my friends' friends . . . but of the

population generally, as seen in town and country, among the rich and the poor, in the slave states, and the free states. I do not like them. I do not like their principles, I do not like their manners, I do not like their opinions. . . .

Late that evening as she paced round the deck she planned exactly what she would do with the money her book would bring in. She had forgotten Nashoba, the Mississippi basin with its "mephitic airs" and brooding forests, Cincinnati with its hogs, its lack of drains, its inimical population. She had even forgotten Trollope's Folly. All those things were past, dead. It was the future that mattered. She threw back her head and saw in imagination, written across the night sky in letters bright as gold, the *Domestic Manners of the Americans, by Mrs. Trollope!*

5

The Laurel and the Thorn

1831-1835

(*i*)

It was a blazing August day when Fanny, Cecilia, Emily and Henry reached home; yet as they stepped across the threshold of the Harrow Weald house all were conscious of a certain chill, a sort of dankness in the atmosphere. The whole place was in a state of neglect. The furniture showed unmistakable signs of mildew, the curtains and carpets were filthy, every room they entered bore a thick pall of dust. Thomas Anthony, looking exceedingly ill, greeted them warmly enough but in the voice a man lost in the desert might have used to welcome his rescuers. In answer to their eager queries of "Where is Thomas Adolphus?" "Where is Anthony?" he waved a lackadaisical hand. Thomas Adolphus was on a walking tour of South Devon and he wasn't quite sure *where* he was at the moment. Anthony had set off early that morning for Vauxhall, where some kind of entertainment was being held, and was unlikely to return before the small hours of the following day. But matters of the gravest import awaited discussion. For example, he must tell Fanny of Dr. Whately's shocking behaviour. . . .

"And how," interrupted Fanny in a tight little voice, "was Anthony going to reach Vauxhall?"

Her husband looked mildly surprised. "On foot. It is a mere fifteen miles or so. But Dr. Whately . . ."

In one quick movement Fanny divested herself of bonnet and shawl. Heaven forbid that she should spoil their reunion by losing her temper, but really the carelessness, the sheer incompetence of Thomas Anthony passed belief! The idea of letting their eldest son wander off without leaving a list of places where he proposed to stop overnight! And just imagine allowing a little boy like Anthony to trudge a full fifteen miles, alone and in the pitch dark, along a road infested by footpads and kindred scoundrels! (Partly owing to her agitation, partly because of her long absence, Fanny quite overlooked the fact that Thomas Adolphus was a man of twenty-one and Anthony a sturdy youth of sixteen.) Most assuredly it was high time she took control of home affairs once more, and as for the house . . . ! Rather sharply she sent the children upstairs to start unpacking, whipped pencil and notebook from her reticule, and began a minute inspection of each room while Thomas Anthony, obstinately refusing to be deflected from his purpose, trailed after her.

As she shook curtains, exclaimed at the depredations wrought by moth, tut-tutted over stains and scars on cherished tables and chairs and jotted down particulars of necessary repairs, he embarked on his monologue of woe. His profound admiration for Dr. Whately's Liberalism had caused him to choose Alban Hall for Thomas Adolphus although it was by no means one of the less expensive colleges and he had therefore to impose the most drastic restrictions on his own expenditure. Alas, his sacrifice had been rewarded by an act so ungentlemanly, so despicable, that at first he had been unable to believe it had truly occurred. It was doubtless right that a Principal should require undergraduates to return after vacation on the exact day set for the opening of term, but when an ailing parent needed his son at home then the rule should, of course, be waived. Now it so happened that at the end of the last Christmas vacation he was prostrate with headache and had delayed Thomas Adolphus's return to Oxford by a day so that the boy might attend to some urgent farm matters. Within a week he received from Dr. Whately a monstrous bill together with a curt, not to say insolent, note informing him that the penalty for his son's lateness was the payment of the enclosed sum to the servant who was porter and buttery man at the hall. Naturally he answered immediately, pointing out that the Principal had acted *ultra vires* in making any such *motu proprio* edict and demanding a full apology. Far from apolgising Dr. Whately had written several rude and violent letters, to which Thomas Anthony had replied with commendable restraint. Finally Whately summoned Thomas Adolphus and told him to take his name off the college books! This Thomas Anthony had at first forbidden his son to do, but when the boy explained that refusal would mean not only the loss of his two Winchester exhibitions but the damning stigma of expulsion, he had realised the detestable Whately held the whip hand and agreed to the ignominious business. Racked by pain—for the affair had had disastrous effects on his health—he had journeyed post-haste to Oxford and laid the full circumstances before Dr. Macbride, Principal of Magdalen Hall (later Hertford College), who showed the greatest sympathy and agreed to receive Thomas Adolphus forthwith, thus saving the precious exhibitions and any imputation of dismissal.

At the beginning of Thomas Anthony's recital Fanny had listened with half an ear, but as its gravity penetrated her consciousness she gave up all attempt to estimate the damage done to the house and sat blinking at her husband in stupe-faction. Had there ever been such a disputatious man? No wonder he had failed as a barrister, failed with Uncle Meet-kerke, failed—here she winced slightly—as a father. Poor, poor Thomas Adolphus, who had suffered such a mischief through his parent's fatal tendency to quarrel with his fellow-men! "Surely you are aware," she said abruptly as Thomas Anthony launched into an eulogy of Dr. Macbride's benev-olence, "that Magdalen Hall has the worst possible reputa-tion?"

"For what?" asked Thomas Anthony rashly.

"Scholarship and discipline," snapped Fanny. "Most of its undergraduates are middle-aged, either *ci-devant* army officers or unqualified schoolmasters who want a degree in order to better themselves. They say that a Magdalen Hall man would as soon aspire to a bishopric as to 'Honours': they say too that if he is locked out late at night there is no need to scale a wall—he simply rings the gate-bell and the porter lets him in."

Thomas Anthony coughed and ran a finger round the in-side of his collar. As he was no match for his quick-witted wife, he hastily reverted to the subject of Whately. Since the *débâcle* he had discovered, to his horror, that that gentleman nursed an insensate hatred for Winchester and had been heard to remark that it was commonly said at Oxford "it was next to impossible to make a Wykehamist believe that any examination could be harder than that which the candidates for New College undergo." Furthermore he had once re-buked Thomas Adolphus (without reason) by growling at him, "We don't want any New College ways here, sir!" An uncouth character in every way. Now Dr. Macbride was a very different man. . . .

Fanny rose, murmuring that it was time the children had

an evening meal, whereupon Thomas Anthony said in an injured tone that he had a great deal more of moment to impart to her. He was considerably disturbed about Anthony, who could neither write a decent hand nor do a simple arithmetical sum after over ten years of schooling. The servant—he had felt it extravagant to retain more than a general handyman—was growing extremely slovenly and needed a sharp reprimand. The purchase and freight of the goods for Cincinnati had swallowed practically the last of his capital and now the financial position was perilous. Then there were the farms. Oh! there were so many things crying out for instant decisions.

But Fanny was already half way down the kitchen passage. Mention of the Cincinnati Athenaeum-bazaar had very nearly destroyed the last vestige of her self-control. How distressingly short of expectation homecoming had fallen! But as she reached the kitchen door she paused and squared her shoulders. There was so much to be done and so little time in which to do it; but that was the sort of challenge which appealed to her.

During the next hour the bewildered servant did more work than he usually got through in a week, and at the end of it he was presented with a week's wages and told to leave the premises before noon the following day. Cecilia and Emily were instructed to unpack and air the household linen while Henry was despatched with a request to a farm labourer's wife to come up in the morning. Fanny herself, armed with broom and duster, attacked the disgracefully dirty bedrooms. It was late before the exhausted family sat down to a cold meal and after it Fanny insisted on the children going to bed. Thomas Anthony's face brightened momentarily—now they could finish their talk. Fanny, however, demurred. There was no time for talk, she said sententiously, when such a lot of action was necessary, and she bustled about so assiduously that presently he said he thought he would retire too as he felt a headache coming on.

It was a relief for Fanny to be left alone. She settled herself at the desk in the morning-room. A mutual friend in America had given her a letter of introduction to Captain Basil Hall, and not a moment must be lost in forwarding it. In her neat script she wrote him a covering epistle complimenting him most sincerely on his book and adding that it had inspired her to set down her own experiences. If it would not be too much of an imposition she would be humbly grateful for his advice on her manuscript. Having sanded and sealed this missive with its enclosure she turned to the absorbing task of correcting the final chapter of *Domestic Manners of the Americans,* but for once she could not concentrate and her glance kept straying to the clock. What ever had happened to Anthony? It was now past two o'clock and there was no sign of him. Pushing back her chair she rose, crossed to the window overlooking the drive, opened it and leaned out. The farm lay bathed in golden moonlight and as a little summer breeze fanned sweetly against her cheek she thought how good, how lovely was this England she had left so long. Presently she heard the sound of footsteps, heavily clumping ones which approached nearer and nearer until the dark squarish figure of their owner came into sight round the bend of the drive.

"Anthony!" called Fanny softly.

The figure stopped, stared at the lighted window, seemed about to shy away.

"Anthony, it's Mama. I'll open the side door for you."

But the figure advanced at a jog-trot. "No need," the voice was rough, even surly, and the next minute Anthony Trollope swung himself over the low sill and faced the mother he had not seen for over three and a half years. "How d'ye do?" he said with a half-nod, half-bow.

She had taken a step forward ready to embrace him; now she hesitated, utterly taken aback by the formality of his greeting. Could this burly young man, this—this stranger, really be the child she had said goodbye to in 1827? He stood, head a little on one side, regarding her quizzically out of bright blue eyes set deep under bushy brows and she noticed with a pang that his jacket, with the too-short sleeves from which his big hands and wrists stuck out, and his trousers, which flapped dustily over his clod-hopper boots, had obviously been handed on to him by his father without any attempt at alteration. "My dear boy," she murmured "you must be worn out. Tell me, what was the Vauxhall entertainment?"

A flicker of animation lit his heavy face. There had been dancing and, better still, some magnificent illuminations and fireworks all provided for a specially reduced entrance fee of one shilling.

"And what did you have for supper?"

He looked at her in astonishment. "Nothing. I only had the shilling."

"D'you mean," cried Fanny indignantly, "that you have had nothing to eat since leaving here yesterday morning?"

He nodded indifferently; whereupon she trotted off to the kitchen and returned carrying a tray laden with cold meat bread, cheese and milk. Watching him wolf the food she knew regret for her long absence from this youngest son and began gently to ply him with questions. Did he like Dr Drury's classes? Had he made many friends at school? What hobbies did he follow during the holidays? But his answers were gruff and unsatisfactory. Indeed, he seemed to resent her interest, the only time when he showed the least response being when she asked him about his thick blackthorn stick with the basket handle. Oh, he and Thomas Adolphus had tremendous bouts with these single-sticks, but he was quicker than his eldest brother and he generally won.

Fanny reflected grimly that she had not come home a minute too soon. Things had reached a pretty pass when young gentlemen fought each other with such murderous weapons, but aloud she said pleasantly that bedtime was long overdue. Standing on tiptoe she put her hands on Anthony's shoulders preparatory to kissing him, but to her mortification he twisted his head so quickly that the kiss landed on the nape of his neck. It was a tiny yet humiliating episode which stayed in her mind as she prepared for bed. And then Thomas Anthony, whom she had thought asleep, began mumbling about farming troubles again. "The farms," she said firmly, "must wait until I have dealt with more urgent affairs." She was not finding it easy to forgive her husband for his deplorable action in destroying Thomas Adolphus's university career or his negligence in allowing Anthony to tramp to Vauxhall looking like a ploughman's son and with only a shilling in his pocket. Strangely enough her thoughts dwelt more on Anthony than on his brother and when sleep came she dreamed she was delivering a lecture on life in America while he stared at her accusingly from a seat in the front row.

(*ii*)

Fanny was delighted when a communication arrived from Thomas Adolphus giving an address in Plymouth and stating that he could find no tobacconist *ex professo* in that city. "I succeeded after some search," he went on, "in getting some tolerable tobacco from a chymist." He hoped to return home by the end of the month and deeply though Fanny longed to see her first-born she was glad to have the opportunity of putting the house in order before the boy's arrival. Two sturdy country girls were engaged and such an orgy of cleaning and washing begun that Thomas Anthony fled to the haven of his study, there to resume work on the compiling of his monumental dictionary of ecclesiastical terms.

According to Anthony's *Autobiography* the Harrow Weald house was a tumbledown old place with little to commend it. According to Thomas Adolphus, who was his mother's life-long companion and champion, it was a perfectly sound building which had acquired a shabby, forlorn appearane during the years it had been left without a woman's care. Perhaps unkindly one is inclined to place more credence on Anthony's description, but there is no doubt that Fanny returned from America to find her home in a shocking state of disrepair. She had, however, an extraordinary effect on the most derelict of houses, caused not so much by her passion for cleanliness as by her gift for impressing her personality on a room. By the end of August the place was transformed into a gracious dwelling where the busiest man or woman could relax, and feel conscious of a sense of tranquillity—yet Fanny herself was surely the least tranquil of beings!

Her spirits rose steadily as she bustled about directing the maids, the village dressmaker who was turning and mending curtains and covers, the french polisher who was restoring the sheen to the furniture. What a joy it was to be home again and what a treat to be among friends capable of intelligent conversation! She had always acted as a social magnet in the Harrow district: now she was regarded as an intrepid heroine and new friends as well as old clamoured eagerly for details of her American experiences. The Drury clan appeared in full force at the weekly "At Homes" she started so soon as the drawing-room was presentable; all her other Harrow friends rallied round, people made special journeys down from London to enjoy her deliciously witty accounts of life in Cincinnati, and the Reverend Mr. Cunningham again hovered on the doorstep.

The reunion with Thomas Adolphus effectively erased memory of the first disastrous day of home-coming. Mindful of the fact that he, Cecilia—who was now eighteen—and Anthony needed the companionship of their contemporaries, she invited numbers of young folk to the house, all of whom were delighted to come. Nobody, they declared, could hold a candle to Mrs. Trollope in the arranging of tableaux, charades, spelling bees and other fascinating entertainments.

Despite this frantic activity Fanny was well started on a second book. The habit of writing so many words a day, begun at the Mohawk cottage, was strictly adhered to and early in September her belief in herself as an author received an added spur. Captain Basil Hall had answered her initial letter with the assurance that he would read her manuscript with interest; now he wrote that he was charmed with a book which supported his own assertions and views so nobly, that he was highly enthusiastic about its chances of success, and that he would gladly do all he could to find a publisher for it. In those days every book about America was looked at from a political party point of view, and Hall had been sorely wounded by what he felt to be savage and unjust attacks on *Travels in North America* by critics belonging to the Liberal party, who accused him of untruthfulness and misrepresentation. In Fanny's book he saw the perfect complement to his own and being a man of generous mind he was determined to help her. He had a considerable literary reputation, and so zealously did he work on her behalf that within a re-

markably short space of time Messrs. Whittaker, Treacher
and Company of Ave Maria Lane, St. Paul's, made her an
excellent offer and said, moreover, that they would use
Auguste Hervieu's illustrations.

Fanny hurried to tell Thomas Adolphus the breath-taking
news. Between this eldest child and herself was a special
bond, one that had strengthened and deepened during the
past few weeks, for he was the only person with whom she
could discuss the private worries she hid so assiduously from
the rest of the world. He had a gentleness of nature, a tol
erance of mind not usually found in a very young man, and
although Thomas Anthony's crazy quarrel with Whately
had destroyed his dream of academic success he showed an
understanding of, and loyalty towards, his father which
moved her strangely. Now it gave her enormous pleasure
to be the bearer of good tidings instead of bad and when he
had congratulated her with fervour she began to chatter
volubly of the vast difference publication of her book was
going to make in their lives.

She knew that the "elementary lectures" provided at Mag
dalen Hall were useless, but he would soon be able to afford
a course of cramming under a private tutor and when he had
taken his degree he could attend a French or German uni
versity. Then there was Cecilia—perhaps her presentation
at a Drawing-room could be arranged; and Henry seemed so
much better that some suitable opening must be found for
him, while Anthony must have extra coaching. Then there
was the house—roomy it might be, but no amount of labour
could make it really habitable and she suspected it was damp
Did Thomas Adolphus remember that solidly built house on
their Northwick estate farm at Harrow, the one they had let
to a tenant when they built the house now occupied by that
wretched "Velvet Cushion Cunningham"? There was th

very place to move to. Even if it had been empty for a year or so, thorough airing and firing would soon put matters right. And dear Papa must be wheedled into an interview with a first-class London doctor. This local man, with his gloomy prognostications, his overdoses of calomel, his irritating way of humming and haa-ing was clearly of no use. After all, the cure of headache was a simple affair to an efficient medico. . . .

Thomas Adolphus grew more apprehensive as her picture of the future grew more roseate. Sensible beyond his years and of a cautious disposition, he was aware of several things which seemed to have escaped her darting glance. He agreed with her views on calomel, but in his opinion Papa's nervous system was so shattered that no treatment could restore it; indeed he often felt his mind was unhinged and to his consternation his mother's presence had not, as it had always done before, lessened the terrible gusts of rage, the ensuing periods of black depression. He knew, moreover, that the annual loss on both farms now amounted to a frightening total, a fact he was certain his father had not disclosed. Worst of all, he had been shocked by the physical change in his brother Henry and felt, like Coleridge with Keats, there was death in his hand. But Thomas Adolphus adored his mother. He had not the heart to tell her that however successful her book proved (and he genuinely believed it would be a best seller) it could remove neither the financial disaster nor the personal sorrow which lay ahead.

So Fanny went gaily on with her plans. She gave several parties for her old friend Miss Mitford, who came on a visit; she made tentative inquiries about Cecilia's presentation; she set about furbishing up the house on the Northwick estate (long afterwards made famous by Anthony as "Orley Farm"); she renewed close friendship with old Lady Milman of Pinner, widow of Queen Charlotte's physician and mother of the Reverend Henry Milman, then famous as poet, dramatist, and "author of perhaps the best Newdegate ever written"; and she began a lengthy correspondence with a German acquaintance, the Baron de Zandt, concerning a post-Oxford course for Thomas Adolphus. According to the Baron, "in many parts of Germany a man may be boarded and lodged comfortably for £26 a year. If he prefers economy to comfort, it might be done for considerably less." At this news Fanny began weaving dreams around Heidelberg University. By dint of reverting to her Cincinnati writing hours she managed to finish her second book, and in no time at all it was Christmas, with Thomas Adolphus at home again together with the delighted Hervieu, who now regarded his dear Mrs. Trollope as a fairy godmother.

Assuredly the new year of 1832 promised well, but two worries still perturbed Fanny's mind. The first was the singular behaviour of Thomas Anthony. The most trivial incident—a chance light remark, a sudden laugh, a tune played on the piano—sufficed to send him into a paroxysm of rage which terrified everybody within sight or hearing and resulted in a headache which prostrated him for three days. In intervals of these attacks he was by turns morose or argumentative. He seemed determined to inflict his moods upon his wife, his children and their guests, for he would stalk into the jolliest party, the most sparkling "At Home" and stand before the fireplace, brooding over the scene like some huge, predatory bird. Occasionally he would growl out such devastating remarks that not all Fanny's social charm could prevent a pall from falling on the company. ("I do not think," wrote Thomas Adolphus sadly, "that it would be an exaggeration to say that for many years no person came into my father's presence who did not forthwith desire to escape from it. . . . Happiness, mirth, contentment, pleasant conversation, seemed to fly before him as if a malevolent spirit emanated from him.") He refused to see a London doctor, refused to believe in Fanny's writings, refused every gesture of help she offered—and she offered many.

Poor Thomas Anthony was at heart the kindliest of men but in this state of chronic ill-health he was acutely conscious of the fact that he was a failure. Intensely proud and fond of his wife, he felt it utterly wrong that she should assume responsibilities he was unable to shoulder, and out of that feeling sprang a wild, unreasoning resentment. He was of no use in the world, nobody wanted him, the only thing he could do was to retire to his study and his *Encyclopaedia Ecclesiastica;* but when he sat hunched over his desk he heard the merry, laughing voices of his family from the drawing-room next door and knew such an aching, intolerable sense of loneliness that he felt compelled to join them. He hated himself for doing so, for his action always brought the same bitter results—the sudden cessation of chatter, the polite responses to his questions, the shadow on every face when he suggested with forced geniality that he should read aloud to them. (Why, thought Fanny desperately, must he choose *Sir Charles Grandison* again?) But Thomas Anthony, hypersensitive as he was, simply *had* to read *Grandison*. It was his challenge, his throwing down of the glove, and as his monotonous voice droned on the children shot longing glances at the copy of Beattie's *Young Edwin* over which they had been having such fun before he came in. . . .

> And yet young Edwin was no vulgar boy;
> Deep thought would often fix his youthful eye.
> Dainties he heeded not, nor gaud, nor toy,
> Save *one short pipe* . . . !

Grimly aware of their boredom, their fidgets, their surreptitious nods and winks to each other, he read on while a thousand devils gnawed at him. They were all against him, even Fanny . . . Ah, no, *especially Fanny,* whom America had changed into a hard, unsympathetic woman so wrapped up in her ridiculous little schemes that she had no time to spare for the sick husband who loved her. By the time Thomas Anthony closed the book and dismissed his family to bed he was so full of self-pity that it flooded out of him as the door closed behind Thomas Adolphus. He was misunderstood, neglected, despised . . . and as she listened to these now painfully familiar ravings Fanny wondered just how long her strength would endure.

Her second worry was Anthony's attitude towards her. Since the night of her home-coming when he had evaded her kiss she had called up every wile at her command and laid siege to his affections. In the friendliest manner possible she had encouraged him to talk of school, of what friends he would like to ask home, of the career he wished to follow when his days at Harrow were over. She had drawn him into every ploy, devised the most exciting excursions, overhauled his deplorable wardrobe and—perhaps because she had a slight sense of guilt—had made a particular point of sharing little secrets with him.

Anthony had not even met her half way; he had failed to respond at all. His answers to her innumerable questions were monosyllabic. He had nothing to say about school, he wasn't very interested in lessons. There were no boys he wished to ask home and he had never thought about what career he would like to take up. He enjoyed the outings she arranged and thanked her for them briefly. He accepted her confidences with mild interest but when she whispered that nobody else knew he simply looked at her blankly and said in his distressingly gruff voice, "Why not?"

Fanny did not, of course, attempt to gain an insight into her youngest son's mind—it is doubtful if she knew he possessed one. As a small boy he had worshipped his gay, amusing Mama from afar because she had always been too busy with Papa, or Thomas Adolphus, or Henry, or Cecilia, or baby Emily to spare him much attention. Then she had suddenly disappeared to America, taking Henry and the two sisters who had been his companions with her, and left him to a life so wretched that he still suffered nightmares about it. Thomas Adolphus and Henry had disliked their father's lessons and Mark Drury's classes bitterly enough, but they had also enjoyed their mother's protection and the happy atmosphere she created in her home; he had crawled wearily from a neglected house dominated by a tyrannical parent to a school where every minute of every day he was forcibly reminded of the fact that he was an outcast. In his loneliness, which grew well-nigh unbearable during his eldest brother's American visit, he had come to believe that he was the one unwanted member in a devoted band of brothers and sisters who basked in the affection of a brilliant mother—and in his secret heart he blamed that mother for ever having borne a child she could not love.

Her return—as sudden as her departure—had thrown him into a state of inner turmoil. On the one hand it had re-awakened all his old longing to stand well in her eyes, to win her smile of praise, her gesture of love; on the other it had revived memory of how she had left him without a backward glance, condemned him to purgatory without a single qualm. Without perhaps being fully aware of his reasons he was suspicious of her every move, from her embrace of welcome to her whispered confidences. His love for her was probably deeper than before—how could he *not* love a mother who transformed the grey stone of life into a shining, iridescent bubble?—yet he vaguely distrusted her, could not believe she loved him in return. He was so different from the others. They were quick-minded, accomplished, comely to look upon; he was stupid, surly-mannered, a clumsy adolescent who never knew what to say or how to manage his too-large hands and feet; so each time his mother reached out to him he instinctively withdrew. He was the odd man out and nothing she could say or do could change that desolate fact.

But Fanny could not penetrate beyond the rough exterior to the tender heart, the searching, sensitive mind. She was not accustomed to having her beguilements thrust aside and in her eyes Anthony was a decidedly difficult, not to say tiresome, boy. Mentally he seemed extremely backward (his handwriting was a positive disgrace) while physically—well, there was only one word to describe his shambling gait, his gruff voice, his general appearance of shagginess, and that was the word "uncouth." It was, however, his attitude towards her, his mother, that disturbed her most of all. When with his brothers and sisters he could talk and laugh in boisterous (too boisterous) fashion, yet the moment he and she were alone together for what she hoped would prove a cosy little talk he backed away from her like a frightened pony. Often too she would raise her head to find him staring at her with a curious, appraising expression in his eyes—in her opinion children had no manner of right to appraise their parents. Of course, he had been left a great deal to himself (she preferred not to remember exactly why) and it was her definite duty to shake him out of his solitary ways; therefore she persisted in her attempts to turn him into what she called a "normal" boy, smilingly called him her "ugly duckling" (she never knew how savagely the nickname hurt), and was considerably upset when she failed to obtain results.

But in the early spring of 1832 the tempo of life was so fast that her anxieties over husband and youngest son faded temporarily into the background. There was the move to the comfortable house on the Northwick estate; there were the proofs of *Domestic Manners of the Americans* to correct; there were scores of friends, both old and new, to entertain. A few months earlier she had met Letitia Landon, at that time famous for the verses she wrote under the initials L.E.L. Her output was prodigious and while her effusions could scarcely be dignified by the name of poetry they were immensely popular among feminine readers of the day and it was rumoured that publishers paid as much as five hundred pounds for the privilege of issuing a dainty, much decorated volume of her sentimental rhymes. It is hard to believe that a woman of Fanny's literary taste really appreciated L.E.L.'s burblings but she was undoubtedly impressed by their success and she was, like many others, intrigued by their author's personality. Very small, with a pointed chin and a turned-up nose, Miss Landon had certain eccentricities which more than compensated for her lack of good looks. In an age when girls were expected to remain under the parental roof and behave with the utmost decorum until some eligible suitor rescued them from bondage, she lived in rooms paid for out of her own earnings, gave parties at which she openly addressed gentlemen as "dear" or "darling," was a witty conversationalist, and entertained male guests, singly and unchaperoned, to tea and muffins.

Even the disapproving were titillated by the delicious flavour of scandal surrounding Miss Landon and were anxious to meet her (just once, of course, and in company); and Fanny, apart from a genuine liking for the poetess, found her a most satisfying visitor. Harrow resounded with stories of her latest *bon mot* overheard at Mrs. Trollope's dinner-table. She had been placed next to an elderly and eminent divine who was said to be more interested in food than in theology and the two had been so absorbed in conversation that someone had asked Miss Landon afterwards what deep subject they had talked about. "About eating, to be sure!" she retorted. "I always talk to everybody on their strong point. I told him that writing poetry was my trade, but that eating was my pleasure, and we were fast friends before the fish was finished!" She had proved a match for the brilliant but terrifyingly erudite Henry Milman, had actually dared argue—yes, *argue!*—over his contention that Dr. Shuttleworth, author of the *Consistency of Revelation with Itself and with Human Reason,* was "a man of very limited reading," and had reminded him that his own family said, "Henry reads a book, not as other mortals do, line after line, but obliquely, from the left-hand upper corner of a page to the right-hand lower corner of the same!" She had also (and this caused Harrow folk to applaud) utterly routed the Reverend Mr. Cunningham when he had tried to interest her in his evangelical beliefs.

As her reputation as a hostess mounted, Fanny had little time to reflect on Thomas Anthony's outbursts or Anthony's difficult behaviour. The ghastly years in America seemed far away, and the joys of a mild and glorious spring added to the exhilaration of her mood. Strolling round the garden with her guests she admired the burgeoning trees and the daffodils starring the grass but she failed to notice the deplorable state of the farm lands beyond. Life was good.

With the coming of high summer life was more than good, for the success of *Domestic Manners of the Americans* exceeded even Fanny's expectations. The Conservative papers lauded it to the skies; the Liberal papers damned it in the bluntest terms; the British public, as eager to know the reason for this violent press controversy as to find out the customs and usages of their trans-Atlantic cousins, besieged the bookshops for copies; the Americans themselves, naturally angered by what they considered a more libellous caricature than that perpetrated by Captain Basil Hall, gave the two volumes such lengthy and savage reviews that every literate adult from New York to New Orleans felt impelled to buy them and the publishers had the greatest difficulty in keeping the supply equal to the demand. Sales mounted, edition after edition was rushed through the press, every journal of note carried controversial letters from admirers or detractors, and very soon it was abundantly evident that Mrs. Frances Trollope had written *the* book of the year.

It was also (although nobody, least of all its author, knew this at the time) the best book she was ever to write and even today, some hundred and twenty years later, the vividness of its descriptions, the biting quality of its wit, make study of it rewarding; but it was by no means a fair, balanced study of its subject. Thomas Adolphus, always his mother's sturdy champion, admitted this long afterwards in his memoirs:

"It was asserted that many of the statements made were false and many of the descriptions caricatured. Nothing in the book from beginning to end was false; nothing of minutest detail which was asserted to have been seen had not been seen; nor was anything intentionally caricatured or exaggerated for the sake of enchancing literary effect. But the tone of the book was unfriendly, and was throughout the result of offended taste rather than of well-weighed opinion. It was full of universal conclusions drawn from particular premises; and not sufficient weight, or rather no weight at all, was allowed to the fact that the observations on which the recorded judgments were founded had been gathered almost entirely in what was then the Far West, and represented the 'domestic manners' of the Atlantic states hardly at all. Unquestionably the book was a very clever one, and written with an infinite *verve* and brightness. But—save for the fact that censure and satire are always more amusing than the reverse —an equally clever and equally truthful book might have been written in a diametrically opposite spirit." (Thomas Adolphus wrote those words in the eighteen-eighties and perhaps his criticism was slightly biased by the fact that years earlier Colley Grattan, author of the very popular *Highways and Byways* and for long British Consul in Boston, had invited his friend to visit him but had added: "I think that to come over under a false name would be *infra dig*. But really I fear that if you come under your own, you may be *in for a dig!*")

The book was, in truth, a remarkable achievement for a woman of fifty-five years old who had never written before and people were not slow to recognise that fact. Letters poured in from all over the world, editors prayed humbly for articles, no less a publishing giant than Mr. Richard Bentley of New Burlington Street came forward with the most handsome proposals for two further books, one on the Belgian people and another on the French. One cannot blame Fanny for basking in so much adulatory warmth: one can only applaud her immediate decision to use her earnings for the good of her family and home and wish she could have been allowed to savour her sudden literary triumph in peace of mind.

But that, alas, was a state she was not to know again for several years.

(*iii*)

In fairness to Thomas Anthony it must be emphasised that since his wife's homecoming he had tried several times to tell her how worried he was about the situation on both the Harrow and Harrow Weald farms. The trouble was that he had either chosen a moment when she was absorbed in some highly important household or social ploy, or approached the subject in such roundabout, garrulous fashion that she lost patience before he reached it, or flown into a rage so stormy that the onslaught of one of his headaches bereft him of the power of speech. Offended by her seeming lack of interest yet conscious that he alone was responsible for the annual losses which now assumed monstrous proportions, the wretched man had nursed his anxiety in secret until Fanny, her bright brain surging with fresh plans, explained to him in detail how she proposed to use her new-found money.

Then the whole miserable story came out. There were debts for this, debts for that. Creditors were clamouring for payment. The goods for the Athenaeum-bazaar had taken the very last of his capital. Bankruptcy lay ahead.

As she listened Fanny's hopes curled and withered one by one—no tutor for Thomas Adolphus, no healthy life on the land for Henry, no London visit for Cecilia. . . . Desperately her mind raced back over fifteen years to the house in Keppel Street, to her arguments about the benefits of a move to the country, to her dreams of a secure, leisured existence at Julians after Uncle Meetkerke had been gathered to his fathers. How wrong all her premises had been! Generous-minded even in adversity she realised now that she had had no right to force poor Thomas Anthony into farming, to make him struggle against floods, droughts, poor soil, tumble-down cottages and fences, labourers with no atom of intelligence, animals that caught the most unconscionable diseases. And America—ah, no, that had not been a mistake, for look what had come out of it! Without a word of reproof she stretched out her hand to her husband and said cheerfully that they would go into all the farm affairs together and see what could be done.

It was quickly apparent that nothing whatever could be done. Certainly with the money coming in from *Domestic Manners of the Americans* and the agreements just signed with Mr. Richard Bentley for further books, Fanny was in a position to keep the family in a far greater degree of comfort than they had known for quite a time; but what was entirely beyond her powers was to pay the farm debts as well. The glorious summer of 1832 faded into a grey winter during which there were endless interviews with legal advisers, interminable conferences with Lord Northwick's agents, with creditors, with tenants. Important though it was to cut losses as soon as possible it seemed that everything conspired to prevent the Trollopes leaving Harrow, but as 1833 dragged on Fanny, who had felt the publicity and consequent humiliation deeply, decided that it was ridiculous to live like a hermit any longer and resumed her "At Homes" and dinner-parties. It was a brave gesture, but it cost her dear. Well-meaning guests frayed her nerves with whispered commiserations, acquaintances asked if she were thinking of selling this tallboy or that wing chair, friends offered advice, temporary homes for the children, even—and this was the last straw—financial help.

Outwardly Fanny remained the perfect hostess who knew instinctively how to make everyone feel at ease. Without

apparent effort she took up the ball of conversation whenever it rolled to a standstill and tossed it into the midst of a
momentarily silent group. Under her adroit management
the shyest girl or young man lost all awkwardness, the most
garrulous bore ceased to dogmatise. Inwardly she was acutely
aware of the curiosity people strove to hide, of their pitying
glances, of their furtive looks towards Thomas Anthony who
brooded, melancholy and hunch-shouldered, over all his
wife's social functions like some black, watchful vulture.

Strangely enough she was completely unaware of an onlooker whose sharp eyes saw and noted every detail of what
was going on; indeed she often upbraided him for his in-
different manners, his clumsiness, his vacant expression when
some older person tried to draw him into a discussion.
"Anthony," she would murmur as she passed him, "don't
slouch," or "Do take your hands out of your pockets," or
"Pray try to *look* interested even if you are not."

Yet the events of 1833 were etched so deep into Anthony's
brain that fifty years afterwards he wrote the whole tragic
story of the Trollope exodus from Harrow as vividly as if it
had occurred only a twelvemonth earlier.

(iv)

When Fanny had first learnt the full extent of her husband's commitments she had declared passionately that she
would work her fingers to the bone rather than allow the
stigma of debt to rest on her innocent children. When it
was gently pointed out to her that if she made herself
responsible for the farms she would be obliged to neglect
those same children, she not only yielded to wiser counsels
but, characteristically, thrust all memory of the fourteen
hopeless years at Harrow into that mental lumber-room at

the back of her mind where she stored unpleasant things. The past was dead, finished with: it was the future that mattered—and she was at pains to emphasise that, thanks to her literary success, it was an infinitely brighter one than the family had hitherto known. Just as soon as the lawyers (why was the law such a tortoise?) had come to some sort of settlement they would move to Belgium where, so she was informed, money stretched a great deal farther than it did in England. There she would write her book for Mr. Richard Bentley while Thomas Anthony worked on his *Encyclopaedia Ecclesiastica* and Cecilia and Emily enjoyed all the amenities of Continental life. Since the moribund authorities of Magdalen Hall had only seen fit to award the scholarly Thomas Adolphus a third-class pass (and that merely on his Latin writing!) he should return to Oxford to attend divinity lectures. Henry should accept dear Fanny Bent's kind invitation to spend several months with her in Exeter, where the pure Devon air would speedily remove the last traces of his chest weakness. Anthony, now eighteen and unfortunately as backward as ever, should sit an examination for a clerkship in the secretary's office at the General Post Office.

Thomas Anthony brightened visibly when he heard this news. He had battled for so long with the hideous spectre of financial disaster and now that it had vanquished him he was content to leave all arrangements in Fanny's capable hands with the soothing prospect of being able to devote himself to his encyclopaedia (he had so far only reached the letter B). The girls too were delighted at the thought of the entrancing new experiences awaiting them and Henry, who was extremely fond of Fanny Bent, looked forward to his stay in her home. His brothers, however, were not so elated. Thomas Adolphus had never quite recovered from the transfer to Magdalen Hall necessitated by his father's quarrel with Whately and could work up no enthusiasm for a course in divinity which, he knew, would be of little use to him. Anthony loathed the idea of clerking in the Post Office and shambled round the house scowling at everyone he met.

Fanny, of course, paid not the least attention either to her eldest son's tentative arguments or her youngest son's mutterings. "Mother knows best!" she said oracularly and sailed off to Belgium, whence she returned in a mood of lyrical enthusiasm. She had leased a charming house called the Château d'Hondt, just outside the St. Peter's, or southern, gate of Bruges. She had met a host of gay, intelligent people in the city, all of whom were eager to meet Cecilia and Emily. And did they remember that pretty Miss Tomkisson, the pianoforte manufacturer's daughter, who had come several times to Harrow parties? Well, she was now married to Mr. Fauche, the British Consul at Ostend, and gave the most amusing parties.

Suddenly the Harrow house was filled with bustle. The Château d'Hondt was unfurnished; so all the Trollope goods and chattels had to be listed, packed and transported across the Channel. The energetic Fanny, darting hither and thither, had also to supervise the overhaul of Thomas Adolphus', Henry's and Anthony's wardrobes and make a hundred and one different arrangements, for Thomas Anthony had already given up interest in anything save his encyclopaedia. She then journeyed to London in search of suitable lodgings for Anthony when he left school the following year, and found a room in a shabby lodging-house in Little Marlborough Street which was owned by a tailor and presided over by his domineering mother. This landlady assured Fanny that none of her "young gentlemen" had any opportunity for backsliding. Her terms were remarkably moderate—probably because few lodgers could endure her iron discipline—and when she reached home Fanny regaled her family with an account of the old lady's eccentricities. "Her laws," she said amusedly, "are as numerous and of the same nature as those of the Medes and Persians"; then she smiled at Anthony's lugubrious face and added she was sure he would be happy in his new home. His protests she dismissed with a wave of the hand—would he *please* not distract her with such foolishness when she was calculating how many nightshirts Thomas Adolphus would require for his term at Oxford? And having settled this and other weighty matters she accompanied Henry to Exeter in order to see him settled in and to discuss with Fanny Bent various questions as to diet and medical care.

In the New Year Thomas Adolphus departed for Oxford and Anthony went to board with Harrow friends. As she scurried round attending to last-minute details Fanny comforted herself with the thought that the three boys were safely housed for at least another six months, though she did feel chagrin at Anthony's surly farewell. But as the coach bearing Thomas Anthony, the girls and herself rumbled towards London she leaned forward eagerly in her seat, chattering about the Ostend packet, the delicious coffee they served in Belgian hotels, the romantic appearance of Bruges. She deliberately refrained from looking out of the window as they passed through the familiar streets of Harrow—she was done with the place and she was leaving it without a pang of regret. Bruges—ah, Bruges was where she should have made her home long ago!

And for the first few months at the Château d'Hondt it really seemed as if she were right. The house was a large and roomy one in which the furniture looked somehow far more imposing than it had done in England. Cecilia and Emily made rapid progress in French and were enchanted with the churches, the graceful buildings, the still canals that gave back reflections yet more beautiful than the originals. Thomas Anthony's health improved both mentally and physically and as he divided his time between working in his room and prowling around ecclesiastical libraries he no longer cast a blight over the many social gatherings which Fanny, who attracted clever, witty people as a magnet attracts iron, was quick to arrange. She made friends in Bruges itself, the Fauches brought the most agreeable variety of acquaintances—mainly musical—over from Ostend, and during the spring and early summer of 1834 it became a positive fashion among literary and artistic folk in London to spend a few days in Bruges so that they might visit their dear Mrs. Trollope.

Towards the end of May Fanny's sense of well-being was heightened by the arrival of her beloved Thomas Adolphus, who had now completed his course in divinity. Together he and she made several little excursions they greatly enjoyed, especially one to a Carmelite monastery where they found the one non-theological book in the library to be a *Cours Gastronomique* which, they felt, was "scarcely needed by a community bound by its vows to perpetual abstinence from animal food," and where Thomas Adolphus was extremely interested in a passage in some folio on casuistry which asked "whether it is lawful to adore a crucifix, when there is strong ground for supposing that a demon may be concealed in the material of which it is constructed?"

These days of holiday were woefully short-lived. Before the middle of June came a letter from Fanny Bent giving a disquieting report of Henry's health and this was speedily followed by another containing the dread news that the Exeter doctors said his lungs were so ravaged by phthisis that they could hold out no hope for his recovery.

Fanny was beside herself with anxiety. Tied as she was to the Château d'Hondt by the needs of Thomas Anthony and the girls she could not go to Devon to be with her son; therefore Henry must somehow make the journey in easy stages from Exeter to Bruges. Once she had him under her own care, she kept repeating, she could nurse him back to health —look at the pitiable state he had been in *twice* during their American sojourn and the wonderful powers of recuperation he had shown! Fanny Bent was not to blame, but doubtless the boy had caught a chill and neglected it, as boys will, and the doctors (who were probably country bumpkins anyway) had made a wrong diagnosis. Hurriedly she sent for Dr. Herbout, an old army doctor who had served under Napoleon, and asked his advice. Partly to soothe her, partly because he was less a physician than a surgeon and knew little about consumption he agreed that Henry should be moved to Belgium as soon as possible.

Within a week Henry was on his way to London, resting frequently at coach stages, and he arrived in Bruges at the end of June in such a shocking state of exhaustion that even Fanny's courage failed her when she looked at him. Not that she admitted her fear to anyone; rather did she intensify her usual gaiety of speech and briskness of mien, but all too soon it was pathetically obvious that Henry was beyond human help. Fretful, yet filled with the optimism which often goes with his complaint, he proved a most difficult patient, demanding his mother's presence at his bedside the day long. For hours at a time he would talk of the places he would like to visit when he was better, the things he would like to do, and she had to smile and agree with all he said until the next dreaded haemorrhage attacked him. For the bewildered Cecilia and Emily she had to invent endless ploys which would keep them out of the sick-room, firstly because they must not be frightened by witnessing their brother's sufferings, secondly—and more tragically—because a Belgian specialist had warned her that little Emily showed every sign of the same malady. Then Thomas Anthony's brief period of normality deserted him and he reverted to his violent rages, his moods of depression, his frequent headaches. Too ill himself to understand that Henry was dying he railed at his wife for what he called her neglect. Why could she not put cold cloths on his throbbing temples as she had always done before? Why had she no sympathy with his suffering? Why did she no longer tempt his appetite with little invalid dishes? Why . . . ? Why . . . ? Why . . . ?

Few women can have passed through more tribulation than did Frances Trollope in the second half of that year 1834. From nine in the morning until eight in the evening she was with Henry, performing the hundred and one nursing chores that had to be done, listening to the plans for future travels that wrung her heart, telling him funny stories, singing for him the nursery songs of Keppel Street days about the "Captain bold of Halifax" and the "unfortunate Miss Bayly," only leaving him to attend to the more urgent of Thomas Anthony's needs or to hold a hurried (and painfully vivacious) talk with the girls about their French lessons, or their friends, or their embroidery. Having settled Henry for the night she had to see to housekeeping matters, listen half asleep to Cecilia and Emily's chatter, and probably endure a diatribe from Thomas Anthony who—thank heaven!—retired exceedingly early and swallowed a nightly dose of laudanum.

About nine at night, when the house was still, Fanny's real day began. She had made a considerable sum out of *Domestic Manners of the Americans,* her novels were proving popular (she could now reckon on receiving about £600 from each), and she had Mr. Bentley's handsome contract, but ever since the publication of her first book two years earlier she had shouldered the responsibility of keeping the entire family and had therefore had no opportunity of saving money. Now that there were large doctors' bills to meet for Henry—and the grim probability of others for his father and sister in the near future—it was absolutely necessary for her to write without pause. Since it was out of the question to do this in the daytime she had to sit down at her desk, utterly wearied in mind and body, and every night until about three in the morning continue to write a novel "calculated to appeal to light-hearted readers," keeping herself awake with innumerable cups of green tea and eventually snatching a few hours' sleep with the aid of laudanum.

Early in September she announced that she must interview her London publishers (a polite fiction since the real object of her visit was to obtain the best possible medical advice for Henry and Emily) and that she would take the invalid and his younger sister because she thought the change of scene might do them good. Thomas Anthony grumbled and Cecilia looked horrified at the idea of being left alone with Papa; whereupon Fanny nodded mysteriously and said that a very kind friend had suggested sending dear Henry on a voyage to Madeira during the coming winter. Surely, she added guilefully, neither Papa nor Cecilia would put any obstacle in the way of her arranging for such a delightful happening?

Naturally they capitulated—though Thomas Anthony wished Fanny hadn't the habit of *always* putting him in the wrong—but unfortunately Henry himself got to hear of the Madeira trip and could talk of nothing else during a journey which drove Fanny almost demented lest he collapse *en route*. Thomas Augustus, who had heroically turned to private tutoring and was lodging in Little Marlborough Street with Anthony, met their boat at Tower Stairs. Alas, the specialist who examined Henry at once vetoed the Madeira idea and said bluntly he doubted if he would live through the return crossing to Belgium, while he shook his head sadly over the state of Emily's lungs.

Worn out and despondent Fanny left Thomas Adolphus in charge of the hotel and trailed to Little Marlborough Street with the intention of congratulating Anthony on his unexpected success in the Post Office examination. To her consternation she was greeted by the tailor's mother, who informed her that the younger Mr. Trollope was not in, that he kept disgraceful hours, and that he was, in her opinion, bound straight for perdition. Sitting bolt-upright on the edge of a chair Fanny waited an hour, two hours, for the prodigal's return. By that time her temper was at boiling-point and poor Anthony, who was genuinely concerned about Henry and feeling full of sympathy for his mother, received a verbal lashing he never forgot his life long.

Next morning the pitiful trio were seen off by Thomas Adolphus on a voyage yet more ghastly than the outgoing one, for Henry was nearly delirious with fever and babbled ceaselessly about Madeira while Fanny stroked his brow and wondered drearily what plausible lie she could invent that would account for the cancellation of the longed-for trip. Had it not been for the kindly help of Mr. Fauche, Henry might never have reached Bruges, but reach it he did and Fanny's treadmill round began again.

As the autumn closed in the Château d'Hondt became a veritable prison. In the spring, with the pale sunshine streaming through its tall windows and its spacious rooms crowded with happy, laughing people it had seemed a charming home: now thick grey mists swirled around it and the only inhabitants walked on tiptoe and a dank unpleasant smell rose from the near-by canal. The capable Fanny of the daytime pretended bravely that things were as cheerful as before, but the Fanny of the midnight working hours, who had no need to wear a mask, found herself trembling at the creak of a board, the scamper of a mouse behind the wainscotting. Every sound, she thought as she forced herself to concentrate on the writing of a sweetly romantic love scene or a piece of brilliantly witty dialogue, had a ghost-like quality. Time and again she laid down her pen, imagining she heard Henry's plaintive cry of "Mama!" or Thomas Anthony's querulous call of "Fann-ee! Fann-ee!" but when she listened intently there was no repetition—nothing but a silence yet more ominous than the fancied voices.

November gave way to December and horror mounted. Weakened by successive haemorrhages Henry lay propped on pillows, his skeleton fingers plucking at the counterpane, whispering an endless monologue on the travels he and Mama would start on next week, or perhaps the week after They would journey toward the sun—he wanted the sun so much. They would see the blue Mediterranean, the golden sands of the North African coast, the wine-dark waters of the Aegean, the fabled cities of the East conquered by his hero Alexander the Great. . . . And when Fanny stole from the room as he dropped into an uneasy doze she had to comfort Cecilia, who was now aware of her favourite brother's condition, and tell Emily some nonsense rhyme while she rubbed her chest, and try to rouse Thomas Anthony from the gloom in which he sat enshrouded. Sometimes she felt her heart so swollen with agony that it must burst within her, but not once did she fail to write her nightly stint of words until December twenty-third. On the morning of that day Henry died.

For the first time in many weeks he awakened without even a slight fever and instead of greeting her with the usual hoarse inquiry as to when they were leaving the cold and damp of Bruges he spoke of arrival at Cincinnati, reminding her with a chuckle of the hogs, the funny hired "Helps" they had had, the day they had all fallen through the rotten tree-trunk in the forest and been bitten and stung by every insect west of the Alleghenies, the time she had been so scared by Fenimore Cooper's tales that wild Indians stalked her in dreams. What fun it had all been, he said, then gave her a radiant smile before falling back on his pillows.

It was the smile that Fanny remembered as she broke the news to the family, talked to the hastily summoned Dr. Herbout, wrote to Thomas Adolphus, made out a list of instructions for the shocked and broken Thomas Anthony; and when the sympathetic little nursing sister from a neighbouring convent came out of Henry's room she murmured her thanks, walked in, and locked the door behind her. All day she sat by the window (she who was never idle) staring dry-eyed at the drifting mist, the words of David echoing and re-echoing through her brain: "O my son Absalom, my son, my son Absalom! Would God I had died for thee . . . !"

The still figure with decorously crossed hands lying on the bed behind her wasn't Henry. Henry was a merry boy with a twinkling eye and an impish gift for mimicry. (*"Nate, nate! Clane, clane!* Do ye mop it, mop it, Mister *Dane?"*) Henry was the gay young man who had acted in amateur theatricals with the Price girls and caused more than one feminine heart to flutter at Harrow parties. Henry had made a joke of their most trying American experiences. Henry had always been the one chosen to approach his parents when there was any wheedling to be done. Henry had smiled at her so gloriously only this morning. . . . "O Absalom, my son, my son!"

It was quite dark when she became aware of repeated rappings on the door. "Fann-ee! Fann-ee!" called Thomas Anthony, "you must not-er-stay there alone, my dear. Are you all right?"

For a moment she was tempted to ask him to leave her alone with her grief; then she sighed, rose stiffly, and lit a candle. She owed a duty to the living as well as to the dead, a duty she must not forget. "I am coming," she answered, and shielding the candle-flame with her hand, she crossed over to the bed. In the flickering light Henry's waxen face seemed tinged with healthy colour and—yes, a smile curved his mouth.

"To lock yourself in!" fussed Thomas Anthony as she opened the door. "Why, it isn't—isn't . . ." he wanted to say it wasn't decent, but the stony look on Fanny's face stopped him and he substituted an even more unfortunate remark. "Why, you might have caught your death of cold! I have made all the arrangements," he hurried on as he armed her downstairs.

"How kind," said Fanny mechanically, and listened while he droned on about the greed of Belgian undertakers, and the Protestant section of the Bruges city cemetery, and the impossibility of Thomas Adolphus arriving in time for the funeral. How old and frail he looks, she thought. And how tired I feel, how very, very tired.

(*v*)

It must be acknowledged that the climate of Bruges could have had little or no effect on Henry who was in such an advanced state of phthisis when he reached the city: it seems almost inconceivable to believe that a mother who had already lost one child should have continued to live with a sec ınd consumptive child and an exceedingly sick husband in a ow-lying house which was next door to a particularly un-ıealthy canal and was wreathed in fog for at least four out of :very twelve months. But that is exactly what Fanny did. Her natural resilience was so strong, her belief in her own :apabilities so great, that once Dr. Herbout had assured her :hat there was no immediate cause for anxiety about Thomas Anthony's condition she saw no reason to leave the Château l'Hondt. In Emily's case she was convinced that good food, plenty of fresh air, and suitable companionship would effect a cure. After all, she confided to Thomas Adolphus, she now had much more time to devote to her younger daughter.

So Emily, her nostrils asasiled by smells and her throat by fog, coughed herself to sleep each night in a room with a wide-open window, and Thomas Anthony, in the intervals he was headache-free, struggled laboriously through the C's in his encyclopaedia, and Cecilia allowed herself to be per-suaded into the enjoyment of little parties again, and Thomas Adolphus relinquished his private tutoring without regret, acted as unofficial secretary to his mother, and squired his sisters' friends round Bruges.

Fanny was delighted to have her eldest son's company and support—she had been highly indignant that a rich widow whose son he coached had complained that he arrived at her Belgrave Square house "in a very dusty condition"—and said he must remain at home until some really satisfactory post offered itself. By the March of 1835 she had begun another novel and had practically completed her book on Belgium. She was also involved in a great deal of correspondence with a Miss Clarke, a friend who had an apartment next to that of Mme Récamier in the Abbaye-aux-Bois, concerning a pro-posed stay in Paris to gather material for a work she wished to call *Paris and the Parisians*. In addition, the spring invasion was again in full swing and one of the most welcome guests from England was Fanny Bent, who had never been on the Continent before and was determined, so Fanny said jokingly, to climb to the top of every tower in Bruges, Antwerp, Brussels and Liége.

In the beginning of April Thomas Adolphus received an exciting letter from a fellow Wykehamist, the Reverend George Hall, offering him the mastership at King Edward's Grammar School, Birmingham, which he himself was about to resign. The salary was £200 a year and since the Head Master was a Dr. Jeune, an old friend of Hall's family, there seemed no doubt that Thomas Adolphus would be elected to the post if he wished. Sad though she was at the thought of losing him Fanny heartily agreed with his decision to return to England at once. He crossed from Ostend to Dover in the *Arrow,* "the only other passengers," so he wrote his mother, "being a maniac and a corpse." Whether this macabre company had any effect on subsequent events we do not know, but he arrived in Birmingham to find the board of governors arguing fiercely about retrenchment and was obliged to return to London and cool his heels in Anthony's lodgings while awaiting their decision.

At that time Fanny was very annoyed with Anthony because she had received distressing reports about his laziness from senior Post Office officials, and there is no doubt she asked Thomas Adolphus to take his brother to task. Perhaps memory of the trouncing his mother had given him the previous autumn still rankled, or perhaps (and this seems more likely) he could not yet forgive her for putting him into the Post Office, but Anthony assumed a mood of open defiance, saying that he hated his job, his lodgings, and life in London, and that he had no intention of doing any more work than he was absolutely obliged to do. Thomas Adolphus was sin-

cerely attached to Anthony but he was also very much under
his mother's thumb and by the time he went up to Oxford to
take his degree on April 29th, she had read between the lines
of his evasive replies to her questions and despatched a letter
to Anthony telling him of her grave displeasure with his
conduct. He took refuge in sulky silence and, sadly enough,
the gulf between Fanny and the son who was so like her in so
many ways, deepened and widened.

Meanwhile, with a sublime disregard for the appalling sani-
tary conditions in Louis Philippe's capital, Fanny had swept
Thomas Anthony and the girls off to Paris where Miss Clarke
had found them rooms at No. 6 Rue de Provence. A mal-
odorous ditch—really an open sewer—ran down one side of
the street, the centre of which was piled high with garbage,
and every drop of water had to be purchased from swarthy
mountaineers from the Auvergne who staggered up the steep
staircases of the houses with buckets of the precious liquid.
Thomas Anthony irritated his wife by repeating *"Lutetia
Parisiorum"* and adding Carlyle's translation—"Mudtoon of
the Parisians," and Cecilia and Emily complained so much
about the stench and the difficulty of washing that she had to
remind them sharply to count their blessings. But these
minor pin-pricks were as nothing compared to the joy of
being in Paris, the centre of art, of culture, of civilisation.
Thanks to Miss Clarke, Fanny at once met both the aristo-
crats of the *ancien régime* and the celebrities of the Quartier
St. Germain and was invited to their houses, and she was en-
raptured when, early on in her stay, Mme Récamier induced
the great Chateaubriand to give a special reading from the
manuscript of his famous work *Mémoires d'Outre-tombe*
especially in her honour. Since most of the Paris notabilities
fought in vain to gain entrance to these readings she was
indeed favoured and on the appointed evening she and the

girls, so excited they could hardly speak, presented themselves
at Mme Récamier's salon in the Abbaye-aux-Bois, Rue du
Bac.

The first part of Fanny's account of the occasion is re-
grettably reminiscent of a present-day gossip paragraph: "The
party assembled at Mme Récamier's on this occasion did not,
I think, exceed seventeen, including Mme Récamier and M.
de Chateaubriand. Most of these had been present at former
readings. The Duchesses de Larochefoucauld and de Noail-
les, and one or two other noble ladies, were among them.
And I felt it was proof that genius is of no party, when I saw
a granddaughter of General Lafayette enter among us. She is
married to a gentleman who is said to be of the extreme *coté
gauche*."

The passage chosen concerned the author's visit to the
royal exiles at Prague and in describing it Fanny shows how
completely she fell under the spell of the man she always re-
fered to as "an aristocrat *jusqu'au bout des ongles*": "Many
passages made a profound impression on my fancy and on
my memory, and I think I could give a better account of the
scenes just described than I should feel justified in doing, as
long as the noble author chooses to keep them from the
public eye. There were touches that made us weep abundantly; and then he changed the key, and gave us the prettiest, the most gracious, the most smiling picture of the young
princess and her brother that it was possible for pen to trace.
And I could have said, as one does in seeing a clever portrait, 'That is a likeness, I'll be sworn to it.'"

But when Thomas Adolphus, who had been told to his
chagrin that the King Edward's governors might go on
wrangling about the appointment of a new master until the
summer term ended, arrived to join his family, and was introduced to Chateaubriand, Fanny was horrified by his ver-

dict on her hero: "He seemed to me a theatrically-minded man."

How, she demanded, dared he say such a thing about the greatest man in France?

Thomas Adolphus answered calmly that he said so because it was true. Chateaubriand was a "tinkling cymbal," and immediately after meeting him he had read his *Génie du Christianisme,* which had confirmed his impression that "he honestly intends to play a very good and virtuous part, but he is playing a part." Probably, the young man went on, too much adulation had gone to his head—but had his mother heard the amusing story of Chateaubriand and his wife, who were supposed to be very short of money? "They put all they possessed into a box, of which each of them had a key, and took from day to day what they needed, till one fine day they met over the empty box with no little surprise and dismay."

To Fanny this was little short of heresy—but worse was to follow, for during some reception she overheard Chateaubriand, who prided himself on his knowledge of English, ask Thomas Adolphus slyly if he would explain the construction of the sentence, "Let but the cheat endure, I ask not aught beside." This her son proceeded to do simply and succintly, but after half an hour of quizzing him on various points the Frenchman still shook a puzzled head. "Perhaps, sir," suggested Thomas Adolphus, "you are not fully conversant with the rules of English grammar?" That night Fanny and her first-born came nearer to quarrelling than they were ever to do again; and curiously it was the volatile, argumentative mother who gave way before the quiet assertions of the gentle son.

The bond between them had always been close; the shock caused by their narrow avoidance of danger strengthened it and for the remainder of his stay in Paris Thomas Adolphus was the rock on which Fanny leaned—and for the first time she, the indomitable one, needed a solid support. Worn to fiddle-strings by the long strain of nursing Henry, distraught with grief over his death, she had known no respite from work, for sheer necessity had driven her back to her desk the night after his burial. Then there was Emily; for all her brave words about "quick cures" she saw only too clearly the growing transparency of the pretty small face, the listlessness that followed each bout of coughing, the tell-tale stains—tiny as yet—on pillows and handkerchiefs. Now there was Thomas Anthony, of whose rapidly declining health an eminent French physician had taken a very grave view, adding that if he had been asked to guess the patient's age he would have said he was well over eighty—and he was only sixty-two! It was a vast relief to talk these troubles over with the serious, twenty-five-year-old Thomas Adolphus, and an even bigger relief to find that he understood and sympathised with a personal problem which was worrying her day and night.

She was grateful to her novels for the money they brought in, but she was under no illusions as to their literary quality. They were light romances written with a verve which thrilled a large number of feminine readers—considering the conditions under which she wrote them the marvel is they were even readable—and nothing more. But having tasted the sweets of *real* success with *Domestic Manners of the Americans* Fanny naturally wanted to nibble from the same delectable dish with *Paris and the Parisians,* and to her alarm the book simply would not take shape. This was all the more terrifying because while Mr. Bentley had expressed his satisfaction with her Belgian manuscript there had been a certain lack of enthusiasm in his letters. It was imperative, therefore, that the new book should be absolutely first class, but the arder she tried to achieve a brilliant passage the duller it became.

She herself ascribed her failure to the constant anxieties which had beset her ever since her return to Harrow, but one feels that while these undoubtedly contributed to her difficulties the root cause of her inability to bring life into the Paris book lay in something entirely different—the fact that she had to have a subject on which she could sharpen the bright claws of irony. America had been the perfect grindstone for this purpose, but how could she turn Paris, a city she adored, into such a revolting object? How could she poke fun at such glorious beings as Mme Récamier, Chateaubriand, George Sand, Lamartine—and, yes, even Louis Philippe? Why, the mere idea was ridiculous; besides, she told her son, grimly, one did not bite the hand that fed one—a remark that surely came oddly from her lips.

Many, many years afterwards Thomas Adolphus indignantly repudiated this description of their mother in Anthony's *Autobiography*: "She loved society, affecting a somewhat Liberal *rôle*, and professing an emotional dislike to tyrants, which sprung from the wrongs of would-be regicides and the poverty of patriot exiles. An Italian marquis who had escaped with only a second shirt from the clutches of some archduke whom he had wished to exterminate, or a French *prolétaire* with distant ideas of sacrificing himself to the cause of liberty, were always welcome to the modest hospitality of her house. In after years, when marquises of another caste had been gracious to her, she became a strong Tory, and thought that archduchesses were sweet. But with her, politics were always an affair of the heart, as indeed were all her convictions. Of reasoning from causes I think that she knew nothing."

A cruel portrait and one, perhaps, which should never

have been penned, but while the Thomas Adolphus of 188
thundered "there is hardly a word of this in which Anthon
is not more or less mistaken" the Thomas Adolphus of 183
was evidently aware of its basic truth, for he took enormou
pains to show his mother important facets of the contempc
rary French scene that she did not know existed, and withou
his help *Paris and the Parisians* (which eventually enjoye
enormous popularity though it was not a patch on *Domesti
Manners of the Americans*) would have been a downrigh
bad book.

Left to her own devices Fanny would have drifted fror
salon to salon meeting the titled, the famous and the ta
ented, piecing together little snippets of information an
spicing them with a hint of scandal, accepting in her strange
gullible way any story anybody chose to tell her. Wit
Thomas Adolphus she found herself wandering outside th
narrow orbit, exploring a Paris beyond her ken.

First he interested her in the remarkable political dram
then being played out, daily and free of charge, in the cit
streets. She had long talked glibly of Monarchists and R
publicans but now she began to realise the wheels within th
wheels. The Monarchists were divided into the *"Parcequ
Bourbon"* partisans who, although they cast longing eyc
back to the days of Charles X and the white flag, were loya
supporters of a king who was at least a scion of the legitimat
breed; and the *"Quoique Bourbon"* partisans who believe
that the monarch should be elected by the will of the peopl
and tolerated Louis Philippe simply because they were te
rified of the evils which Republicanism had already brough
—and given the least encouragement would bring again—t
their country. In direct opposition to these two groups wer
the Republicans and to add to the general comic opera effec
all three factions togged themselves up in the most astonish

ing uniforms. The *"Parceque* Bourbon" men were the smartest, for their dress was a modified replica of that once worn by the true Bourbon soldiers. The far larger *"Quoique* Bourbon" party—mainly composed of shopkeepers who had joined the immensely popular National Guard—presented the oddest sight, for some stalked about in full regimentals while others contented themselves with wearing ordinary black suits with military shakos, and quite a number merely girded on a sabre round their indubitably civilian waists. But it was left to the Republicans to provide the picturesque touch, for half of them swaggered around in the tricorne hat and greatcoat with exaggerated lapels made famous by Napoleon Bonaparte, while the other half draped themselves in black Spanish cloaks surmounted by sombrero hats.

Being a woman, Fanny was naturally intrigued by the Republicans, but her admiration for their melodramatic if sinister behaviour evaporated after a scene "staged" by them at the Porte St. Martin when they unfurled a huge red flag and shouted that neither the National Guard nor the Legitimists could break their ranks. The challenge was not accepted; instead an ancient fire-engine drawn by two decrepit horses appeared. The elderly driver climbed down stiffly from his seat, unhooked a hose-pipe, and in the most nonchalant manner possible directed a jet of cold water at the disturbers of the peace who promptly fled in wildest disorder.

But when Thomas Adolphus endeavoured to explain to her that the Parisians had good grounds for fearing the Republicans Fanny stared at him in wonderment and said she didn't believe a word of it. Why, M. Thiers and M. Guizot had both told her that they were a stupid, undisciplined mob just playing at being conspirators! It was useless to remind her that the real danger lurked in filthy alley-ways where no gentlewoman—or man either, for that matter—ever dared penetrate, or to talk of the afterglow of Bonapartism that still lingered in the European sky. She had given her heart to the elegant historian-politicians she had met in different salons and as Anthony truly remarked, "with her politics were always an affair of the heart."

Poor Thomas Adolphus! he must have winced when he found she had left out all mention of Cousin in her exposition of French political literature during the eighteen-twenties, and when he came across certain of her references to Thiers; but he must also have known pride when he read a more reasoned passage dealing with contemporary French letters, for in it his own influence on his mother's judgment was noticeable:

"The active, busy, bustling politicians of the hour," she wrote, "have succeeded in thrusting everything else out of place, and themselves into it. One dynasty has been overthrown, and another established; old laws have been abrogated, and hundreds of new ones formed; hereditary nobles have been disinherited, and little men made great. But amidst this plenitude of destructiveness, they have not yet contrived to make any one of the puny literary reputations of the day weigh down the renown of those who have never lent their voices to the cause of treason, regicide, rebellion, or obscenity. The literary reputations of Chateaubriand and Lamartine stand higher beyond all comparison than those of any other living French authors. Yet the first, with all his genius, has often suffered his imagination to run riot; and the last has only given to the public the leisure of his literary life. But both of them are men of honour and principle, as well as men of genius; and it comforts one's human nature to see that these qualities will keep themselves aloft, despite whatever squally winds may blow, or blustering floods assail them. That both Chateaubriand and Lamartine belong rather to the imaginative than the *positif* class cannot be denied; but they are renowned throughout the world, and France is proud of them. The most curious literary speculations, however, suggested by the present state of letters in this country, are not respecting authors such as these. . . . The circumstance decidely the most worthy of remark in the literature of France at the present time is the effect which the last revolution appears to have produced. With the exception of history . . . no single work has appeared since the revolution of 1830 which has obtained a substantial, elevated, and generally acknowledged reputation for any author unknown before that period—not even among all the unbridled ebullitions of imagination, though restrained neither by decorum, principle nor taste. Not even here, except from one female pen, which might become, were it the pleasure of the hand that wields it, the first now extant in the world of fiction [the allusion is to George Sand] has anything appeared likely to survive its author. Nor is there any writer, who during the same period has raised himself to that station in society by means of his literary productions, which is so universally accorded to all who have acquired high literary celebrity in any country. . . .

"There are, however, little writers in prodigious abundance. . . . There is scarcely a boy so insignificant, or a workman so unlearned, as to doubt his having the power and the right to instruct the world. . . . To me, I confess, it is perfectly astonishing that any one can be found to class the writers of this restless clique as 'the literary men of France.' Do not, however, believe me guilty of such presumption as to give you my own unsupported judgment as to the position which this 'new school,' as the *décousu* folks always call themselves, hold in the public esteem. My opinion on this subject is the result of careful inquiry among those who are most competent to give information respecting it. When the names of such as are best known among this class of authors are mentioned in society, let the politics of the circle be what they may, they are constantly spoken of as a pariah caste, that must be kept apart.

" 'Do you know ——?' has been a question I have repeatedly asked respecting a person whose name is cited in England as the most esteemed French writer of the age—and so cited, moreover, to prove the low standard of French taste and principle.

" 'No, madame,' has been invariably the cold answer.

" 'Or ——?'

" 'No; he is not in society.'

" 'Or ——?'

" 'Oh, no! His works live an hour—too long—and are forgotten.' "

Greatly to Fanny's distress she found that Victor Hugo, whom she much admired, was classed as one of the *décousus*: "I have never," she wrote, "mentioned him or his works to any person of good moral feeling or cultivated mind who did not appear to shrink from according him even the degree of reputation that those who are received as authority among our own critics have been disposed to allow him. I might say that of him France seems to be ashamed. 'Permit me to assure you,' said one gentleman gravely and earnestly, 'that no idea was ever more entirely and altogether erroneous than that of supposing that Victor Hugo and his productions can be looked on as a sort of type or specimen of the literature of France at the present hour. He is the head of a sect, the high priest of a congregation who have abolished every law, moral and intellectual, by which the efforts of the human mind have hitherto been regulated. He has attained this pre-eminence, and I trust that no other will arise to dispute it with him. But Victor Hugo is NOT a popular French author!' "

Then she was taken over the Palais de Justice by "an able lawyer who holds a distinguished station in the *cour royale.* Having shown us the chamber where criminal trials are carried on, he observed that this was the room described by Victor Hugo in his romance, adding, 'He was, however, mistaken here, as in most places where he affects a knowledge of the times of which he writes. In the reign of Louis XI no criminal trials ever took place within the walls of this building, and all the ceremonies as described by him resemble much more a trial of yesterday than of the age at which he dates his tale.' "

It is good to record that Fanny continued to champion Victor Hugo. But she was more intrigued, perhaps naturally, by the appearance, personality and behaviour of that remarkable woman George Sand. Fanny admired the "large eyes *à fleur de tê*," the expressive, mobile mouth, the way she tilted, both in speech and writing, at various windmills; but she did not altogether approve one of George Sand's escapades during that summer of 1835. The Abbé de Lamennais, an aged, wizened little priest who wielded much influence despite the fact he was so dirty that few could bear to sit close to him, was the object of vigilant supervision on the part of Louis Phillipe's police. These gentlemen were no less interested in George Sand, so when she and the Abbé suddenly left Paris together on a country excursion they were assiduously trailed. To the chagrin of authority no subversive activities were reported, and all the watchers had to tell was that the lady and the Abbé shared the same bedroom! It seems highly unlikely that either affection or economy was the motive behind this strange happening. In all probability it was planned with the sole idea of shocking Louis Philippe's minions and showing them that writer and priest were above pandering to conventionality, but after hearing of the episode Fanny never felt quite the same towards George Sand again.

On the other hand she steadfastly refused to believe any of the malicious tales concerning Mme Récamier, reiterating stoutly that she was a truly good and virtuous Christian woman, and she also made firm friends with the beautiful Princess Belgiojoso, at whose house she spent many memorable evenings. The Princess was a musician of no mean order, and on one occasion she and Liszt entertained the guests by playing, on two pianos, the whole score of Mozart's "Don Giovanni." This feat did not upset the Princess in the slightest, but as the last note was struck poor Liszt, overcome by nervous strain, slid from the piano-stool on to the floor in a dead swoon!

It was in the same salon that Fanny heard, from the lips of a prominent politician, this remarkably accurate forecast of French events: "You know," he said, "how devoted all France was to the Emperor, though the policy was somewhat tight, and the conscriptions heavy. But he had saved us from a Republic, and we adored him. For a few days, or rather hours, we were threatened again by the same terrible apparition. The result is that four millions of armed men stand ready to protect the prince who chased it. Were it to appear a third time, which heaven forbid! you may depend upon it, that the monarch who should next ascend the throne of France might play at '*le jeu de quilles*' with his subjects and no one be found to complain." (Thomas Adolphus said that in her own copy of *Paris and the Parisians* he found she had written "*Vu et approuvé*, Dec. 10th, 1853, F.T." in the margin of the final sentence.)

But all too soon it was time to think of the return to Bruges. Thanks to her own indefatigable efforts and the help of

Thomas Adolphus she had now collected sufficient material for her book, and reluctant though she was to leave her adored Paris she knew she must write up her observations while they were fresh in her mind. As a farewell to the many friends of different nationalities she and the children had made, she arranged a large picnic party to the beautiful woods of Montmorency. The weather was glorious, the conversation was scintillating, and Fanny was just preening herself on the success of the day when a half-dozen or so young men—led by Thomas Adolphus—declared it was impossible to leave without organising a race on the famous Montmorency donkeys. Among the party who entered this competition with zest was an English youth the Trollopes had just met, William Makepeace Thackeray; and so urgently did he urge his strongly conservative mount into a pace it had never before attempted that the animal suddenly stopped dead and tossed its rider clean over its long ears. Unfortunately Thackeray fell head first on to a heap of newly broken stones, and the alarmed Fanny at first feared for her guest's life. After much bathing of the victim's head, however, it was found that with one exception his cuts were superficial—but the exception left a scar on Thackeray's face which remained throughout his life and he was heard to say more than once that Trollopian parties were scarcely to be recommended.

(vi)

Two members of the family left Paris without regret. Thomas Anthony had detested every moment of his stay there, had found it impossible to work in the noisy Rue de Provence, and had been extremely indignant with Fanny for making him see so many doctors. Poor frail Emily, who was so small and light one could hardly believe she was eighteen, had been positively dazed with exhaustion before she had been in the city a week; and for the remainder of the visit she had begged Mama to allow her to rest while she, Cecilia and Thomas Adolphus spent their evenings at glittering parties. But her pleadings had not always been successful—it was inconceivable to Fanny that a young girl should actually *want* to miss a reading by Chateaubriand or a pianoforte solo by Liszt—and more often than not Emily had been obliged to sit for hours bolt-upright on the edge of an ottoman thinking longingly of her cool, comfortable bed.

Once at the Château d'Hondt Thomas Anthony retreated to his study while Emily lay on the sofa by her bedroom window, but neither of them knew peace of mind or body. The July days were stifling, the nights humid, the effluvium which rose from the canal well-nigh unendurable. It is doubtful whether Emily realised she had not much longer to live, but she fretted constantly because she didn't feel able to join Cecilia and her friends in different little ploys and Fanny's brisk suggestions about short walks and fresh air drove her to weak tears. Thomas Anthony, however, knew that he was dying—had known it for some time—and he struggled frantically, pathetically, over his encyclopaedia. It was, he felt, most humiliating to be beholden to his wife for everything, and he dreaded the thought that when he was gone his contemporaries would shake their heads and say, "Ah, poor fellow, what a tragic failure he was!" Wretched and in pain he shuffled round his room, wishing he could consult this or that authority, visit ecclesiastical libraries, cross to London to confer with old New College friends. But such ideas were out of the question, for he must work on in stuffy, airless Bruges with the woefully inadequate means he had managed with difficulty to collect—and he had only just reached the letter D.

Meanwhile Fanny was in one of her most high-spirited moods. She was working very hard on her book but she found time to make several journeys to Ostend with Thomas Adolphus by "Torreborre's" barge. This barge which was drawn by two horses left Bruges at six in the morning and the fare, including as much excellent coffee and bread and butter as the traveller chose to consume, was one franc ten centimes, and what pleased Fanny was that she could sit on the comfortable cabin roof and write undisturbed. Once Ostend was reached there were the hospitable Fauches to be visited, and a Count Melfort—whom Fanny called a *"ci-devant* Don Quixote sort of a looking man"—and his young wife, and a wealthy Colonel Dickson who was a great connoisseur of food and wine and had been known on one occasion to rush into his drawing-room a few moments before dinner and cry despairingly to his guests, "Great heaven! the cook has cut the fins off the turbot!" A day, or a day and a night, in Ostend acted like a tonic, for though Fanny kept up her cheerful mien before her invalids at home she was intensely worried about the pair of them.

As the summer faded to autumn and the mists once more wreathed the Château d'Hondt in grey draperies Thomas Adolphus set off on another journey to Birmingham, determined this time to get some sort of definite answer from the governors of King Edward's. But no sooner had he left Bruges than Thomas Anthony collapsed. Dr. Herbout was summoned and told Fanny there was little anyone could do; so for the second year in succession she wrote by night and nursed the dying by day. Henry had been a fretful patient: Thomas Anthony was a yet more exacting one, but as she tended him Fanny was amazingly gentle with his rages, his outbursts of self-pity, his reproaches, his pathetic apologies for his own inadequacy, and as she sat at her desk in the small hours her thoughts drifted from *Paris and the Parisians* to the Heckfield rectory and the masterful way Thomas Anthony had wooed her. Such excitement it had all been—the making of the trousseau, the choosing of the Keppel Street furniture, the first dinner-parties to legal luminaries. . . .

"Fan-*nee!* Fan-*nee!*" called the querulous voice, and as Fanny bent above her husband she wept for the years that had gone, realising fully and for the first time how her impulsiveness, her lack of tolerance, her sharp tongue must have irked this man on whom misfortune after misfortune had fallen.

Thomas Adolphus returned on October 15th with the news that no master would be appointed to King Edward's until the fine new school then in course of construction was finished but also with Dr. Jeune's assurance that he and nobody else would eventually get the appointment; and on the afternoon of the 23rd his father died. His grave was close to that of Henry, in the town cemetery outside the Catherine gate, and of his funeral the eldest son wrote, "When I followed my mother to the grave at Florence many years afterwards, my thoughts were far from being as painfully sad, though she was, I fear, the better loved parent of the two. She died in a ripe old age after a singularly happy, though not untroubled life. . . . It was otherwise in the case of my father. He was, and had been for many years, a very unhappy man. . . . I do not see what concatenation of circumstances could have made him happy."

Within a few weeks Fanny had given up the gloomy Château and left Belgium for England. All her care was now concentrated on Emily, for the specialists she had consulted had given the opinion that she might survive in the more bracing airs of her native land.

Henry had gone, Thomas Anthony had gone. . . . Surely the dear God would spare Emily?

The Perfect Partnership

1835-1848

(i)

AFTER a little search Fanny rented a pleasant house standing in its own garden on Hadley common, near Barnet, and into this she moved with the girls and Thomas Adolphus. But no sooner had the family settled down than it became all too evident that Emily was gaining no benefit from the change of climate, and before the end of the year she too was dead. "Her youngest child," wrote Thomas Adolphus, "had ever been to my mother as the apple of her eye, and her loss was for the passing day a crushing blow. But, as usual with her, her mind refused to remain crushed, any more than the grass is permanently crushed by the storm wind that blows over it. She had the innate faculty and tendency to throw sorrow off when the cause of it had passed. She owed herself to the living, and refused to allow unavailing regret for those who had been taken from her to incapacitate her for paying that debt to the utmost."

All the same it took every atom of Fanny's resilience to overcome her sorrow at this last, most poignant tragedy.

Emily had been such a bright, *espiègle* child, full of fun and possessing her mother's high spirits. Hervieu had done a portrait of her, sitting at a writing-desk clad in a brown holland pinafore. Pushed to one side of the desk was a neglected copy-book bearing the legend, "Study with determined zeal!" but the flaxen-haired small Emily with the wide-set china-blue eyes was concentrating all her energies on the blowing of an iridescent soap-bubble. This picture hung in Fanny's work-room and a hundred times a day she found herself glancing up at it.

Fortunately Fanny had the inestimable boon of Thomas Adolphus' company—there seemed little chance of his Birmingham appointment materialising for another twelve months—and with the coming of the New Year romance began to bloom between Cecilia and John Tilley, a fellow clerk of Anthony's at the Post Office. Determined to dissipate the atmosphere of grief which had hung around them for so long Fanny filled the house with gay young visitors, asked innumerable friends down from London to stay, and busied herself with the planning of theatricals, dances, charades and picnics. Freed from nursing duties and able at last to afford capable servants she now altered her writing hours—but five o'clock each morning saw her at her desk and the production of her long series of novels (she wrote in all a hundred and fifteen volumes, though the first was not begun till she was past fifty!) never ceased.

A frequent visitor was the celebrated surgeon Joseph Henry Green, who was introduced by his brother-in-law, Mr. Hammond, another surgeon practising at Hadley. Mr. Green was the possessor of a most lively wit and was, moreover, Coleridge's literary executor, but apart from him, the Hammonds and the family of Mr. Thackeray, the local rector, the Trollopes made few acquaintances in the district,

possibly owing to Fanny's ludicrous experience when returning the call of a rich distiller's wife. This lady was enormously stout and when her guest was ushered into the
drawing-room she said, "Excuse me, ma'am, if I keep my
chair, I never *raise*. But I am glad to see you—glad to see
anybody."

Mrs. Fauche from Ostend came to Hadley for a fortnight,
during which Fanny arranged several delightful little con-
certs, and another visitor from beyond the Channel was an
elderly lady who was an exceedingly strict Roman Catholic.
One day at luncheon she took a great fancy to an oyster soup
which made its appearance and begged that the recipe might
be copied out for her. "Oyster soup!" she exclaimed. "Just
the thing for a Friday!" but when she read the recipe she
was horrified to find the first line ran, "Take of prime beef
two pounds. . . ."

In the spring Thomas Adolphus went to Normandy for
some three weeks and Anthony (still very much the odd man
out) stayed at the Hadley house for a brief spell. He and
Fanny were both on their best behaviour, but their guarded
politeness did not endure. She simply could not understand
why he was so difficult about his work or why he disliked that
admirable landlady, the tailor's mother in Little Marlborough Street. He refused to enter into explanations concerning the natural antipathy existing between himself and
his chief, Sir Rowland Hill, and merely said in a surly voice
that he hated being badgered either in the office or at his
lodgings. Fanny then held up Thomas Adolphus as the shining example of courtesy and gentleness, whereupon Anthony
—who had a real affection for his brother but envied him his
life of leisure—was stung into remarking that he doubted if
Thomas Adolphus would "ever earn his salt in the routine
work of a profession, or any employment under the authori-

tative supervision of a superior." It was not to be expected that Fanny would accept such criticism of her beloved first-born and there were several acrimonious exchanges before a letter from Mr. Richard Bentley distracted her thoughts in a more pleasant direction.

The publisher was immensely pleased with *Paris and the Parisians* and suggested to his dear Mrs. Trollope that instead of carrying out an idea she had put forward of undertaking an Italian tour, she should write a book entitled *Vienna and the Austrians*. Fanny was charmed and since Mr. Bentley's offer was a most generous one she promptly abandoned her arguments with Anthony and sat down to work out details of the proposed trip with such vigour that on Thomas Adolphus' return she was able to greet him with the news that she, Cecilia, and, of course, himself were leaving for Vienna within a month.

Naturally he was delighted at the prospect, for he loved travel and had long wanted to visit Austria. But what about his forthcoming appointment to the mastership at King Edward's in Birmingham? With typical disregard for such minor matters Fanny answered that if the school governors suddenly decided to make up their stupid minds, their failure to secure her son's brilliant services would be a just punishment for their dilatoriness. Surely Thomas Adolphus realised that it was absolutely necessary he should accompany her as courier on this important journey? Besides, she proposed to take Hervieu as well, since his illustrations to both her Belgian and French books had been much applauded, and while he was a wonderful companion he suffered an inability to look after tickets, baggage or money.

Thomas Adolphus capitulated without further demur (his remonstrance had been half-hearted in the first place), and immediately surrounded himself with an astonishing array of maps and guide-books, while Cecilia sewed busily and Fanny's nimble brain thought of yet more exciting ideas. Why didn't Thomas Adolphus ask one of his Oxford friends to join the party? And really she herself would be so engrossed in gathering material that the presence of a maid would be the greatest comfort—that nice woman who had been with them at Harrow for years would be the very person. . . .

The truth was that for the first time in more than twenty years Fanny was without any harassing encumbrances and was enjoying a feeling of emancipation which went to her head like wine.

(*ii*)

The first part of the journey was comfortable enough, for the party travelled by coach through Metz, Strasbourg and Stuttgart; but since Fanny was anxious to see as much of the country and its people as possible they had changed at the German frontier into the incredibly slow *Lohnkutscher,* which progressed at the rate of about thirty miles a day, made unscheduled stops of unpredictable duration, and jolted off the set route to isolated villages in the most inconsequential fashion. By the time Ratisbon was reached the maid was in a state of hysteria (for the remainder of the trip she was never seen without a bottle of smelling-salts) and a ruffled Fanny inspected with very mixed feelings the barge on which they proposed to sail down the Danube to Vienna.

"We start tomorrow, and I can hardly tell you whether I dread it or wish for it most. We have been down to the river's bank to see the boat, and it certainly does not look very promising of comfort. But there is nothing better to be had. It is a large structure of unpainted deal boards, almost the whole of which is occupied by a sort of ark-like cabin erected in the middle. This is very nearly filled by boxes, casks, and bales; the small portion not so occupied being provided with planks for benches, and a species of rough dresser placed between them for a table. This we are given to understand is fitted up for the express accommodation of the cabin passengers."

Fortunately they proved to be the only passengers—indeed Fanny quickly found out that nobody except the local peasants, who sometimes did the short passage between one village and another, ever dreamed of travelling by barge; and that she and her companions were objects of the greatest curiosity to everyone with whom they came in contact. Nobody could believe that the English, always reputed to be enormously rich, ever travelled in such a way, and at every landing-place crowds of people jostled each other in an attempt to glimpse these mad foreigners.

"But the worst thing I saw," wrote Fanny ominously, "is the ladder which, in case of rain, is to take us down to this cabin of little ease. It consists of a plank with sticks nailed across it to sustain the toes of the crawler who would wish to avoid jumping down seven or eight feet. The sloping roof of the ark is furnished with one bench of about six feet long, from which the legs of the brave souls who sit on it dangle down over the river. There is not the slightest protection whatever at the edge of this abruptly sloping roof, which forms the only deck; and nothing but the rough unslippery surface of the deal planks, of which it is formed, with the occasional aid of a bit of stick about three inches long nailed here and there, can prevent those who stand or walk upon it from gently sliding down into the stream. . . . Well! we have *determined,* one and all of us, to navigate the Danube between Ratisbon and Vienna; and I will neither disappoint myself nor my party from the fear of a fit of vertigo, or a scramble down a ladder."

But Thomas Adolphus was equally determined that his mother and sister should enjoy as much comfort as possible. "At a very early hour," wrote Fanny, "T. was up and on board, and perceiving by a final examination of the deck, its one giddy little bench, and all things appertaining thereto, that we should inevitably be extremely uncomfortable there, he set about considering the ways and means by which such martyrdom might be avoided. He at last got hold of the *Schiffmeister,* which he had found impossible yesterday, and by a little persuasion and a little bribery, induced him to have a plank fixed for us at the extreme bow of the boat, which we can not only reach without difficulty, but have a space some nine or ten feet square for our sole use, on condition of leaving it free for the captain about five minutes before each landing. This perch is perfectly delightful in all respects. Our fruit, cold meat, wine, bread and so forth are stored near us. Desks and drawing books can all find place; and in short, if the sun will but continue to shine as it does now, all will be well."

Small wonder that the crew looked up from their oars in amazement, or that news of these extraordinary folk travelled ahead to the next stopping-place. But Fanny beamed from her perch upon crew and villagers alike. She was learning a lot about the countryside and was enjoying her odd voyage—although she did murmur to Cecilia that it belonged to the category of those things which might be done—

> Could a man be secure, that his life should endure
> As of old, for a thousand long years. . . .

Each night was spent ashore in some local and usually primitive inn, and while everybody else complained bitterly about the discomforts they had to suffer Fanny remained steadfastly cheerful until they reached the small Bavarian village of Pleintling. Here their sleeping quarters were so infested with bugs that as soon as it was light the party hurried back to the barge, leaving Thomas Adolphus to settle with the surly landlord. Realising that it would be futile to haggle he paid the man the sum which had been agreed upon the previous night, whereupon he was told he owed more than double that amount. Naturally he refused to pay and walked towards the river, but just as he was about to step aboard the barge the landlord seized him by the throat, shouting that the thieving foreigner had not settled his bill. Hervieu and the other young man of the party jumped ashore to rescue their friend, but were tackled by several nasty-looking customers, while the enraged landlord, who was carrying an axe, lifted this awful weapon and announced he was going to cleave Thomas Adolphus' skull in half! The horrified Fanny screamed for the captain and begged him to pay her son's assailant whatever he demanded. The captain paid and saved the situation but the episode shook Fanny considerably and thereafter she was not quite so enthusiastic about their nightly resting-places.

At last the barge reached Vienna and Fanny's first glimpse of the city so moved her that as the customs officer was examining her baggage she recited to Cecilia the old folk song, *"Es ist nur ein Kaiserstadt, es ist nur ein Wein!"* But unfortunately at that very moment the man unearthed from her hand-bag a pack of playing-cards and asked in a voice of thunder why she was trying to smuggle such a thing into the capital. The startled Fanny explained that she had forgotten the cards were there and she added airily, "Throw them away, or, if the regulations demand it, we will pay the duty though we have not the least desire to retain possession of them."

This suggestion did not please the officer at all. She had been guilty of a serious offence against the law and the only possible way to placate authority was to write a long report as to how the playing-cards came to be in her baggage and to add to this a humble petition for forgiveness on the grounds of her lamentable ignorance of Austrian regulations. Fanny listened in alarm to this oration. It would be too dreadful if she were not allowed to enter the city she had come so far to seek, but the trouble was that neither she nor any other member of the party had sufficient knowledge of German to couch any kind of petition in that language. Haltingly, and with a wealth of gesture, she pleaded so pathetically to the official that suddenly he capitulated, wrote out the petition himself, disappeared with it into an inner sanctum, and came back with the news that it had been granted. Amid sighs of relief the pack of cards was ceremoniously burnt and a relieved Fanny tripped out, a free woman, into the streets of Vienna. Two weeks later she was besieged by invitations from the aristocratic Viennese—the greatest tribute to her charm she ever received in the course of a long life.

True, she had already been received in Parisian salons; but Paris society prided itself on being cosmopolitan and she had been introduced to it by such influential people as the Lafayette family and Miss Clarke. Vienna society was the most exclusive in Europe, a tight little group of nobles who all knew each other's pedigrees and quarterings. The latter were so important that Fanny, blessed with a retentive memory, read them up and learnt them off by heart and refused to know anybody who did not belong to the *grand monde*. Few of them were intellectual—as a rule their conversation verged on the frivolous—but they were elegant to a degree, beautifully mannered, and extremely hospitable towards those whom they chose to accept as friends.

Fanny was fascinated by this tiny world in which ladies never wrote notes but communicated with their friends by sending footmen with verbal messages; and every young man retained in his special pay a public hackney coach which he expected to find awaiting him at any hour of the day or night. She was impressed by the way everybody still told stories of their adored "Vater Franz," who had been succeeded as Emperor by the imbecile Ferdinand two years earlier. "Vater Franz" had set aside a certain numbers of hours every Thursday during which he received any subject, however humble, who had requested speech with him. He refused to allow guards to be present at these interviews and ignored all warnings that he might well be assassinated by some mad nihilist or socialist or "other description of radical." When he had been confined to the palace even with a bad cold the bright Viennese sky clouded over, and when he was able to drive again through the streets he was greeted by crowds of poor folk who actually poked their heads in at the carriage window to assure themselves that their beloved Emperor had fully recovered from his indisposition. And she was especially intrigued by the superb contempt with which these people regarded worldly wealth. Some were very rich, some equally poor, yet no feeling of embarrassment marred their intimacy; and there was one elderly single lady who attended every function but as she could not afford a conveyance she arrived on foot carrying her evening slippers and an extraordinary turban she always affected. These she would hand graciously to a flunkey, and then stand unconcernedly in some splendid entrance hall while she divested herself of her wraps, changed her shoes and adjusted her headdress.

The Trollopes and their friends had been but a matter of

days in the city when they were invited to dine by Sir Frederick Lamb, the British Ambassador, and to Fanny's unbounded delight her dinner-partner was none other than Prince Metternich. He was growing old and the day of his power over Europe was waning, but he was still the undisputed leader of Vienna society. On Fanny, who had been his ardent admirer for a quarter of a century, he exerted an influence so profound that she forsook the Liberal convictions drilled into her over many years by Thomas Anthony and became a staunch Tory.

Both Metternich and his lovely wife, the Princess Melanie, took a great fancy to the lively, observant Englishwoman and throughout the months she stayed in Vienna she was a constant guest at their home. Whether the occasion was an elaborate banquet for thirty or forty people or an informal family dinner she was always placed at her host's right hand, a signal honour which brought her many opportunities of listening to his reminiscences, for owing either to a personal whim or some digestive disturbance he dined in the middle of the day and could thus devote all his time to whatever lady was sitting next to him. A figure of immense dignity with shining silver hair and delicate, high-bred features, he would talk throughout the long meal, occasionally nibbling a thin slice of brown bread and butter from the supply set before him.

As was natural his monologues usually concerned the adversary he had fought so long, the Emperor Napoleon Bonaparte. One of the worst features about dealing with the man, Metternich declared gravely, was that he was not a gentleman in any sense of the word. His manners were "those of the guard-room rather than of the council-chamber" and he deliberately created violent scenes in order to cow his opponents—a method frequently successful but a dead failure when applied to an enemy with sixteen unblemished quarterings. For example, in the celebrated interview when Austria refused to declare war Napoleon lost his temper, snatched off his tricorne hat and threw it into the corner of the room "evidently expecting that I should pick it up and present it to him; but I judged it better to ignore the action and the intention altogether, and his Majesty after a minute or two rose and picked it up himself."

Fanny listened enthralled. Like many of her generation she thought of Napoleon as a monster and pleaded with the Prince for more stories of his fearful behaviour. These were gladly told and the following one, her favourite, she recounted in full in her book:

"During the hundred days of Napoleon's extraordinary but abortive restoration, he found himself compelled by circumstances, *bon gré mal gré* to appoint Fouché minister of police. About ten days after this arch-traitor was so placed, Prince Metternich was informed that a stranger desired to see him. . . . The Prince recognised him as an individual he had known as an *employé* at Paris. But he now appeared under a borrowed name, bringing only a fragment of Fouché's handwriting, as testimony that he was sent by him. His mission he said was of the most secret nature, and in fact, only extended to informing the Prince that Fouché was desirous of offering to his consideration propositions of the most important nature. The messenger declared himself wholly ignorant of their purport, being authorised only to invite the Prince to a secret conference through the medium of some trusty envoy, who should be despatched to Paris for the purpose. The Prince's reply was, 'You must permit me to think of this.' The agent retired and the Austrian minister repaired to the Emperor, and recounted what had passed 'And what do you think of doing?' said the Emperor.

" 'I think,' replied the Prince, 'that we should send a confidential agent, not to Paris, but to some other place that may be fixed upon, who shall have no other instructions but to listen to all that the Frenchman, who will meet him there, shall impart, and bring us faithfully an account of it.'

"The Emperor signified his approbation; 'And then,' continued the Prince, 'as we were good and faithful allies, and would do nothing unknown to those with whom we were pledged to act in common, I hastened to inform the allied sovereigns who were still at Vienna, of the arrival of the messenger, and the manner in which I proposed to act.' The mysterious messenger was accordingly dismissed with an answer purporting that an Austrian, calling himself Werner, should be at a certain hotel in the town of Basle, in Switzerland, on such a day, with instructions to hear and convey to Prince Metternich whatever the individual sent to meet him should deliver. This meeting took place at the spot and hour fixed. The diplomatic agents saluted each other with fitting courtesy, and seated themselves *vis-à-vis,* each assuming the attitude of a listener.

" 'May I ask you, sir,' said the envoy from Paris at length, what is the object of our meeting?'

" 'My object, sir,' replied the Austrian, 'is to listen to whatever you may be disposed to say.'

" 'And mine,' rejoined the Frenchman, 'is solely to hear what you may have to communicate.'

"Neither the one nor the other had anything further to add to this interesting interchange of information. . . . They separated with perfect civility, both returning precisely as wise as they came.

"Some time after the imperial restoration had given way to the royal one in France, the mystery was explained. Fouché, *ette revolution incarnée,* as the Prince called him, no sooner saw his old master and benefactor restored to power, than he imagined the means of betraying him, and accordingly despatched the messenger, who presented himself to Prince Metternich. Fouché was minister of police, and probably all the world would have agreed with him in thinking that if any man in France could safely send off a secret messenger it was himself. But all the world would have been mistaken, and so was Fouché. The Argus eyes of Napoleon discovered the proceeding. The first messenger was seized and examined on his return. The minister of police was informed of the discovery, and coolly assured by his imperial master that he would probably be hanged. The second messenger was then despatched by Napoleon himself with exactly the same instructions as the envoy who met him from Vienna, to the effect that he was to listen to all that might be said to him, and when questioned himself, confess, what was the exact truth, that all he knew of the mission on which he came was that he was expected to remember and repeat all that he should hear."

Under the spell of Metternich's precise, courteous voice, delighted to have her own views on the dreadful Corsican confirmed by a statesman so famous, Fanny gave no thought to the other side of the medal. She could visualise neither the tragic exile at Elba waiting for the arrival of his wife and son, nor the glittering Congress of Vienna where the faithless Marie Louise danced tirelessly with kings and diplomats while Metternich, Talleyrand and Castlereagh re-arranged the map of Europe. She knew only that the greatest man in Austria had given her his confidence and she was downright angry with Thomas Adolphus when he insisted on taking her long walks through Vienna so that she might observe the strange variety of characters from the different countries in the empire. She could not work up much enthusiasm for outland ishly garbed Croatians or Transylvanians; she regarded the Hungarian gipsy encampments outside the city walls as the most unsavoury places she had ever seen; she considered the swaggering Bohemian waggoners and the caftaned Jews from far Galicia as definitely sinister, and so soon as she could she escaped from these tiresome excursions and returned to bask in Metternich favour.

She did, however, consent to the making of a few friendships outside of the charmed circle; for while it was unheard-of for the exclusive Viennese to mix with lesser mortals it was perfectly in order for a foreigner to do so, and many of her *grand monde* acquaintances were so curious to know how this or that renowned artist lived that they begged her to find out. To do her justice she was nothing loth to do so because, Metternich apart, the vapid chatter she heard at receptions and dinners was beginning to pall.

In this way she met Mme Rettich, the very gifted actress who was the first to play the part of Goethe's Gretchen; and the venerable pianist John Cramer, to whom she took an instant liking. He had just finished a monody dedicated to the memory of Malibran, and of it Fanny wrote: "It is full of feeling, and, as I listened to this veteran pianist, as he performed for me his simple and classic little composition, and marked the delicacy and finish of his style, unencumbered by a single movement in which the conceptions of a harmonious genius are made to give way before the meretricious glory of active fingers, I felt at the very bottom of my heart that I was *rococo*, incorrigibly *rococo*, and that such I should live and die."

But as the summer passed Fanny spent more and more time in the company of Princess Metternich, who had kindly consented to allow Hervieu to do a portrait of her with the proviso that Mrs. Trollope was present at every sitting. Between the two women a very real bond of affection developed and rather to her surprise Fanny, who had imagined the Princess to be a frivolous-minded, laughter-loving beauty, discovered that she possessed serious opinions on many subjects; discovered too that while she sincerely loved her husband she held decidedly individual political views of her own. This latter fact rather shocked Fanny to start with, but as the intimacy between them deepened so did her admiration for the Princess' strength of character and she was unboundedly grateful for her help in one particular matter.

Prompted by Princess Metternich the Archduchess Sophie had sent Fanny a gracious intimation that she would grant her an interview on a certain evening. Fanny had a bad cold at the time which resulted in erysipelas, and to everybody's consternation two days before the date of the audience her head was swollen to nearly twice its usual size! The Princess drove to see her immediately and insisted upon taking her to her own personal physician, an elderly homoeopathist who had been Hahnemann's favourite pupil. Told he had to make the patient presentable within forty-eight hours he threw up his hands and declared the task impossible, but under persuasion from Princess Melanie he achieved the desired object and Fanny duly made her curtsey to the Archduchess.

Life in Vienna was so enchanting that Fanny developed ideas about settling there and it was a severe blow when a letter arrived for Thomas Adolphus stating that the King Edward's school governors in Birmingham had at long last made up their minds and decided to appoint him assistant classics master the following January term. Since it was then nearing the end of November and the weather severe it was decided he had better start on the long coach journey as soon as possible lest the hazards of winter travel cause delays. A seat was booked in the coach which carried the imperial mail to Munich, Paris and London, but before he left he and his mother had the privilege of watching a scene of gorgeous pageantry—the installation of eleven Knights of the Golden Fleece.

A second expedition, especially planned by Thomas Adolphus, was not so successful, for he took Fanny to see the huge, long-disused catacombs under the cathedral church of St. Stephen. These had not been used as a burial place for about sixty years, but peculiarities of soil and atmosphere had prevented the processes of decay and to Fanny's horror she had to pick her way between "monstrous confused heaps" of mummified bodies, most of which had been thrown into the catacombs uncoffined and unshrouded during the plague of 1713. Sight of this ghastly charnel-house upset Fanny so much that it effectively removed her sorrow at her beloved son's departure and the writing of a chapter on it (chapter forty in her book) kept her busy until well after Christmas.

Presently, of course, she forgot the awful vaults and again enjoyed herself in Vienna society. But even this seemed to lose some of its charm now that Thomas Adolphus was no longer by her side and early in 1837 she decided to return to Hadley. The parting from the Metternichs and others was bitter indeed, and all through the tedious journey she kept recalling the sparkling brilliance of the Viennese, the magnificent strength of the Austro-Hungarian Empire. Perhaps it was as well that nobody had ever repeated to her "Vater Franz's" prophetic remark: "My nation is like a worm-eaten house; if one part is moved one cannot tell how much of it will fall."

The Indomitable Mrs. Trollope

(iii)

At first Fanny found it both pleasant and soothing to be back in her own home. She greatly enjoyed entertaining all her old friends and it was fun to drive up to London in a hackney coach and attend soirées and routs where she made a host of new acquaintances. Mary Russell Mitford came on a visit and they had long and interesting discussions on the advisability of writing for this or that magazine, Miss Mitford saying emphatically, "as for Fraser's and Blackwood's, they are hardly such as a *lady* likes to write for!" (a remark which rings curiously in present-day ears). As always the companionship of Miss Mitford stimulated Fanny, who found it delightful to be told: "How glad I am to find that you partake of my great aversion to the sort of puffery belonging to literature. I hate it! and always did, and love you all the better for partaking of my feeling on the subject. I believe that with me it is pride that revolts at the trash. And then it is so false; the people are so clearly flattering to be flattered. Oh, I hate it!" though she was not so sure her friend was right when she advised her to write fiction only because "I have not a doubt that that is by far the most profitable branch of the literary profession."

Nevertheless she worked hard at a new novel, aware that the £600 it would bring was not to be scorned. But her heart was with *Vienna and the Austrians* and into these two volumes she put an immense amount of work. By the summer of 1837 she was actually refusing invitations and allowing Cecilia to run the house while she sat at her desk, grey goose quill scampering across the paper in an effort to keep pace with the thoughts which crowded her brain. Her industry was rewarded. Mr. Bentley was highly enthusiastic and when the book was published it was so well received that there was no doubt she would be asked to write a similar work on some other country.

On the surface life seemed satisfactory indeed. She was making an income more than ample for family needs; Cecilia was now formally engaged to John Tilley; tragedy no longer hovered on the doorstep—yet for the first time in her life Fanny was thoroughly depressed.

Little worries that formerly she would have brushed aside assumed ridiculous proportions. Hadley was a dull place and the neighbours a witless lot. Anthony was behaving in most annoying fashion, neglecting his work, quarrelling with his chief, hinting darkly that he was going to apply for a change of job. In another year Cecilia would have gone off to her new life, leaving her mother entirely alone. Thomas Adolphus was unhappy in Birmingham, where he was forced to teach a great many stupid boys who had never heard of Winchester traditions and thought only of making a fortune in some hardware factory.

Fanny had never been good at making allowances for others: now she made none for herself. She did not realise that she was mentally and bodily worn out, or that owing to force of circumstance she had grown into a Matriarch who unconsciously resented her children's natural wish to lead their own lives. Most important of all she had never, unlike most middle-aged people, been aware of "Time's wingéd chariot" rushing past her down the wind until the spring of 1838 when a letter from Princess Metternich brought the sudden, awful knowledge that she had only a handful of years left in which to do all the things she planned.

In itself the letter was entirely innocuous. The Princess had pleaded that in exchange for Hervieu's portrait of herself she should receive one of Fanny by the same artist. This had been completed and sent to Vienna in the charge of a

Baron Hügel. *"Vous ne pourriez croire, chère Mme Trollope,"* wrote the Princess, *"combien le portrait que vous avez chargé le Baron Hügel de me remettre m'a fait de plaisir!*

"Il y a longtemps que je cachais au fonds de mon cœur le désir de posséder votre portrait, qui, interressant pour le monde, est devenu précieux pour moi, puisque j'ai le plaisir de vous connaître telle que vous êtes, bonne, simple, bien veillante, et loin de tout ce qui effroie et eloigne des reputations litéraires. Je remercie M. Hervieu de l'avoir fait aussi ressemblant. Et je vous assure, chère Mme Trollope, que rien ne pouvait me toucher aussi vivement et me faire autant de plaisir que ce souvenir venant de vous, qui me rappelera sans cesse les bons moments que j'ai eu la satisfaction de passer avec vous et qui resteront à jamais chères à ma mémoire."

As she read the letter Fanny was swept by an aching sense of nostalgia, but as she paced up and down her room remembering the sights, sounds and scents of Vienna her mood changed to one of rebellion. Why should she, who was the intimate of the Metternichs, Mme Récamier, Chateaubriand, Thiers, Guizot and countless others, waste her days in Hadley? Why should she, who had walked through the splendid, spacious salons of European capitals, fritter away her time in getting up charades for local charities? The thing was absurd, not to be thought of! She would give up her house, take a little *pied-à-terre* in London, ask Mr. Bentley for another commission—and so soon as Cecilia was safely married she would go abroad again. . . . But as she began to enumerate the places she *must* visit she gave a little shiver and stood still in the middle of the floor. This time she would have to travel alone! And since the far-off day when she had married Thomas Anthony she had never been alone, not for a single moment.

To be alone, always alone. It was a hideous thought snaking through the mind and she, the woman who had faced hardship, disappointment, poverty, disease and grief with indomitable courage, knew that the mere prospect of loneliness would defeat her utterly.

She hated the knowledge—she had no patience with such weakness—and did her best to forget it by weaving the most grandiose plans for the future. Formerly this method had proved a sure anodyne; now it failed completely. Cecilia, unaware of the inner anguish her mother was undergoing, watched her behaviour with astonishment at first, then with alarm. For Mama, most methodical and hard-working of beings, to neglect her writing and leave her desk in a shocking state of untidiness was bad enough; but for Mama to dodge upstairs whenever the front-door bell rang—hissing over her shoulder that she was not at home to *anybody*—was quite incomprehensible. Rather timidly, for while she loved her mother she had always been a trifle afraid of her, she asked if there was anything wrong; whereupon Fanny snapped her head off and, instead of laughing off her momentary anger in the usual charming way, stalked out to the kitchen and gave notice to an excellent and blameless cook. It was all very puzzling and when Anthony came down one week-end Cecilia sought his advice.

Anthony had kept his rough manner, but he was burlier, more boisterous than before, and he had developed the habit of straddling in front of the fireplace with his hands thrust deep into trouser-pockets. Now he eyed his sister thoughtfully as she explained how irritable and restless their mother had become. Perhaps, he suggested with a quirk to his mouth, she missed her marquises or archduchesses, or perhaps she felt lost without her faithful squire . . . ?

At the precise minute Fanny swept into the room.

"Squire?" she demanded sharply, "what squire?" Without waiting for an answer she went on, "Anthony, kindly stop jingling the coins in your pockets—a most irritating sound. And must you really stand in such an undignified attitude?"

Anthony straightened obediently and smiled at her. "Poor Mama," he said softly.

"How dare . . ." began Fanny, then faltered. It was very strange but Anthony's whole expression had altered, his blue eyes were full of sympathy, his smile gentle as a woman's. Involuntarily she took a step forward. . . .

"Oh, Mama," said Cecilia, "there is a letter for you from Thomas Adolphus."

The spell was broken, and after Fanny had left the room clutching the precious missive in her hand Anthony poked the fire thoughtfully. He knew so much more about Mama than she dreamed he knew, and he hoped the letter would make her happy.

Anthony was right: half an hour later his mother came down to dinner in the highest spirits.

(*iv*)

On the 19th of June Thomas Adolphus returned from Birmingham and for the next few days Fanny and he did little else than perambulate round and round the garden, their heads close together, their tongues clacking steadily. The letter Fanny had received on the occasion of Anthony's visit had given her a new and wonderful idea, for in it her eldest son had confessed that he "felt himself unfitted for the duties of a policeman among these turbulent Birmingham lads" and that he was extremely unhappy at St. Edward's. Why, she now argued, should he return there in September? And out tumbled all her plans for the future.

The Perfect Partnership

The production of novels was a never-ceasing labour she was only prepared to undertake if she could vary it by the writing of more travel books. Mr. Bentley was willing to pay handsomely for these travel books, but she felt she could not face the long journeys involved without the guidance and companionship of Thomas Adolphus. His constant presence, indeed, was absolutely necessary if she were to execute all the schemes she had in mind. There was no question, of course, of taking up *all* his time—there would be ample opportunity for him also to take up a literary career and, after all, it need only be a temporary arrangement. If he wished to return to school-mastering he could do so.

Very sensibly Thomas Adolphus pointed out that tempting though the proposition was, its acceptance was tantamount to abandoning, not deferring, any hope of a professional career. He was twenty-eight years old, he had no means of his own, and he disliked the idea of being a burden on his mother. The eager Fanny waved these objections aside. She felt sure literature was his true *métier*, he would receive the same salary she would have to pay a secretary, and since Cecilia and Anthony were not in need she would make over to him the property settled on her by Thomas Anthony at the time of their marriage—the only capital saved from the Harrow disaster.

Thomas Adolphus could argue no further. He adored his mother, he truly detested his Birmingham work, and he was an inveterate wanderer who could think of no more glorious life than one of drifting from country to country at will. Besides, like many young men of his age, he was convinced that he could write. Fanny was so moved when he said he would agree to all her suggestions that she burst into tears, a rare occurrence with her; she then celebrated the start of what proved to be a perfect partnership by falling suddenly and seriously ill.

There is no mention of the nature of her complaint in any Trollopian memoirs. It may have been some purely physical ailment, but one is inclined to think that it was aggravated, if not caused, by the severe emotional strain under which she had been living for several months. There is no doubt that the thought of the lonely years ahead had been almost unendurable and very likely the relief caused her taut nerves to snap. In any event she made a rapid recovery and rose from her bed in a brisk bustling mood which reminded her family of the old days on the Harrow farm. The Hadley house must be given up at once, so would Cecilia please start washing and packing the china, silver and glass? Mr. Green, the surgeon, had mentioned there was a house vacant at 20 York Street, St. James's (a *very* good neighbourhood) so would Thomas Adolphus please journey up to London and find out all particulars about it? She herself would list the pictures and furnishings (packers were so notoriously careless), and the gardener could come in and lift the carpets and the maids could sew sacking round chair and table legs.

Fanny was an expert remover and she also possessed the most extraordinary flair for finding a house exactly when and where she wanted one. Within a week she was standing in the hall at 20 York Street directing the men about the disposal of her belongings and when she sat down to dinner that evening, exhausted but happy, she announced she had made a resolution to write ten post octavo pages of her new novel between the hours of five and eight each morning.

Soon the York Street house was crowded with guests and during the autumn Fanny gave a series of small dinner parties to which she invited a varied assortment of people. A frequent visitor was Judge Haliburton of Nova Scotia, large genial man who wrote humorous books and was therefore known to the world as Sam Slick, the Clockmaker; and the Irish Colley Grattan and his wife came several times, for Fanny never tired of hearing Grattan advising her more erudite and superiorminded guests to write novels. "Fiction, me boy," he would roar across the table at some scandalised don, "fiction and passion are what readers want!"

In February 1839 Cecilia married John Tilley, who had been appointed Post Office surveyor for the Lake District, and thereafter Anthony derived a certain sardonic amusement from watching "Mama and her squire" (as he called Fanny and Thomas Adolphus) succumbing to the craze for what were then called "magnetic *séances.*" A Frenchman, Baron Dupotet, was the most popular magnetiser of the day and Fanny, always the most gullible of women, found his experiments thrilling in the extreme for he not only sent people into trance but actually threw a young woman into convulsions as well! Less spectacular, but probably far more trustworthy, was a Dr. Elliotson, a qualified physician and a friend of Colley Grattan's, who treated cataleptic cases by hypnotism and was obliged to leave a London hospital in consequence. His two most talked-of patients were the Okey sisters, aged about twelve and fourteen, whom he had been treating for a considerable time. They also had to leave the hospital because they were in the habit of pointing to some other patient and crying that they "saw Jack" beside his or her bed. The trouble was that when they "saw Jack" the patient pointed to invariably died!

It was unfortunate that Fanny believed implicitly in the Okey girls, for by a coincidence one of them was a frequent visitor to Anthony's landlady and during that same spring Anthony developed a severe illness which for a time baffled the doctors. He was at his worst when the Okey child, meeting Fanny on the stairs, piped up that she had seen Jack by Mr. Trollope's side, but only up to his knee which meant that he would recover. After that, of course, Fanny practically adopted the Okeys, much to the disgust of the convalescent Anthony.

But soon she was lured in a very different direction by the eloquence of Lord Ashley (afterwards Earl of Shaftesbury) on the subject of factory reform, and promptly decided to write a novel about the appalling conditions prevalent in Yorkshire and Lancashire factories. The book was to be published by Mr. Colburn—who "paid a long price for it"—in the then newly-invented fashion of separate monthly numbers, and was to be called *Michael Armstrong*. Armed with letters of introduction from Lord Ashley, Fanny and Thomas Adolphus set off for the north of England on a tour which provided her with information so horrifying that she sat up half each night writing in a white-heat of fury that such things could be—though strangely enough she never seems to have made any comparison between them and the conditions she had so deplored in the Mississippi basin.

By way of a little relaxation they then paid a visit to the Lakes where they found Cecilia settled into her new home at Penrith, and were very nearly drowned in Lake Windermere because Fanny would insist on going sailing with the intrepid Captain Hamilton, author of *Cyril Thornton*, a best-seller of the day. The high-light of their visit, however was when they received an invitation from Wordsworth to spend an evening at his home. He was waiting in his garden to greet them and after courtesies had been exchanged Thomas Adolphus happened to see a remarkably fine bay tree growing by the front door. "How surprising to see such a luxuriant tree in this exposed position," he said. The poet rounded on him immediately. "Why should you be sur prised?" he growled. Thomas Adolphus stammered that he had thought the bay tree required more sunshine than it could find in the Lake District. "Pah!" snapped his infuriated host. "What has sunshine got to do with it?"

The worried Fanny did her best to pour oil on troubled waters but without much success. Throughout the evening Wordsworth ignored both Thomas Adolphus and Herbert Hill, Southey's nephew, who was also passing the evening there, and addressed a monologue to her concerning the greatness of himself and his works. Since he wore a large green eye-shade and muttered into his waist-coat all the time it was extremely difficult to hear what he was saying, and the only time the members of the party perked up was when he recited, with exquisite expression, his own lines on Little Langdale. At ten o'clock he bade them an abrupt goodnight and as they stumbled through the dark garden Thomas Adolphus asked his mother what all the monologue had been about. "Himself," she said tartly, and added, "maunderer!" In her opinion not even a lion of Wordsworth's stature had any right to bore his audience.

(v)

Fanny returned to York Street, there to finish *Michael Armstrong*, but before she settled down to work she prevailed upon Mr. Colburn to send Thomas Adolphus to Brittany for the purpose of writing a book on that part of France. Since he had only written articles before he would not expect more money than would cover his expenses, she pointed out guilefully, and she further assured the publisher that any "polishing" the manuscript required would be done by herself. Mr. Colburn agreed, mainly because he dared not offend an author of Frances Trollope's standing, and

Thomas Adolphus set off in high feather while the naughty Fanny chuckled to herself in York Street. Now that she and her eldest son were in permanent partnership she did not in the least mind a temporary separation; moreover she was determined that he should eventually take her place in the world of letters. Cecilia had no literary gifts and as for Anthony—Fanny sighed and twirled the grey goose quill in her fingers. Poor Anthony had started life as a clerk and doubtless he would remain a clerk until he died.

Thomas Adolphus returned brimming over with enthusiasm—and his mother noted approvingly that he had spent only a fraction of Mr. Colburn's expense money. Before the pair of them enchanting vistas opened; they had no responsibilities, no cares; they could wander where they willed; that amiable body of men, London's publishers, were only too anxious to finance them. In the autumn, they decided, they would go to Paris for several months, then perhaps to Bavaria to stay with the Baron and Baroness de Zandt, or to Italy . . . but why look so far ahead? they would go where the fancy took them.

At the age of fifty-nine Fanny began to live, fully and gloriously, for the first time in her life, and assuredly she deserved this late reward. From November 1839 to May 1840 she rented a Paris apartment, renewing her friendships with Mme Récamier, Chateaubriand, Miss Clarke, attending operas and theatres, collecting around her a host of new acquaintances who never ceased expressing their admiration for her brilliant wit, appearing as a favoured guest at ambassadorial receptions—yes, and even at Louis Philippe's dull dinner-parties.

On return the York Street house seemed very small, the atmosphere of London stifling, and Fanny quickly decided to rid herself of any permanent home. (It was still such a delightful adventure to be able to shed responsibilities at will.) But since she was incapable of making such a move without indulging in some quite transparent subterfuge she called Thomas Adolphus into conclave and suggested they should go through all the household books. Since she was now making a large income there was absolutely no need for financial retrenchment, but she professed herself horrified by the amount of money they had spent on food. Thomas Adolphus pointed out that she had entertained considerably and that "little dinners" were apt to lead to big bills, where-upon Fanny made a remark he never afterwards allowed her to forget. "The fact is," she said emphatically, "that potatoes have been quite exceptionally dear."

So because of the extortionate price of these humble vege-tables the York Street house was given up, the furniture stored, the trunks packed. Fanny sailed off triumphantly to spend the remainder of the summer with Cecilia, and Thomas Adolphus went on a walking-tour in northern France. But it was a bad summer. The view from Cecilia's house consisted of a curtain of mist rather reminiscent of the view from the Château d'Hondt and by October Fanny was on her way to Bavaria, there to winter with the de Zandts. In the following April she was joined by Thomas Adolphus and the two set off for Italy, as Mr. Bentley had commissioned Fanny to write a book entitled *Visit to Italy*. "Our flying visit," wrote Fanny, "was very pleasant"—although she spent ten months in the country and had previously considered two or three months ample time to gather material! Florence appealed to her particularly and, as usual, she met everybody of interest in that city. In the autumn she and Thomas Adolphus moved on to Rome where they proposed to re-main until the late spring of 1842; but in January they received news from Penrith that Cecilia was expecting her first child, information which threw Fanny into a state of extreme agitation. It was out of the question, so she told her son, for the baby to be born unless *she* was present, and although he explained patiently that owing to severe weather most of the passes were blocked she insisted upon setting forth by diligence early in February.

It was in truth a terrible journey. At Susa, where the snow was falling heavily, they met the descending diligence and its driver sang out happily to Fanny, *"Vous allez vous amuser joliment là haut, croyez moi!"* a statement which caused even the brave Fanny to quail. Grimly she sat back in her corner as the driver urged his poor, stumbling horses up the Mont Cenis in a blinding blizzard and twelve strapping peasants walked alongside to help push the coach at intervals. But worse followed at the top of the pass, for here she was told that the descent must be undertaken on sledges. For one moment she faltered; the next she was the matriarch *in excelcis*. Marching forward she took her seat in the horrible contraption, closed her eyes and prayed for death. The prayer went unanswered, but it was a nightmare ride she never forgot.

(*vi*)

Fanny's matriarchal mood persisted (perhaps memory of the sledge had something to do with it) and shortly after the birth of her grandchild she announced to a startled Thomas Adolphus that she proposed to build a house near Penrith—indeed she had already purchased a site, a hillside field overlooking the ruins of Brougham Castle and the confluence of the Eden and Lowther rivers. He mistrusted the whole scheme, but being an obedient son interviewed surveyors and builders, superintended their work and tried to keep pace with his mother's grandiose plans for beautifying the surrounding land. Her mind full of gardens seen in Tuscany, Fanny purchased hundreds of flowering trees and shrubs, which poor Thomas Adolphus had to plant with his own hands, and then conceived the idea of building a cloistered walk along the entire top of the field. This, she said, would provide shelter from the north winds and the rain, and would make a charming ambulatory from which one might see a magnificent view, while the pillars supporting its roof would be smothered in climbing plants.

While her son toiled and moiled at Carlton Hill—as the house was to be named—Fanny spent much time with friends of her son-in-law's, Sir George and Lady Musgrave of Edenhall. Of ancient lineage Sir George was the proud possessor of the "Luck of Edenhall," a decorated glass goblet bearing the legend:

> When this cup shall break or fall,
> Farewell the luck of Edenhall.

He was also a country gentleman of the old school, who never went to London because he thought his proper place was on his own land, and who was adored by everyone in the countryside. Lady Musgrave held the even stronger view that Cumberland and Westmorland were the only worthwhile counties in England and in support of this contention she affected the speech of the district, always alluding to a cow as a "coo."

Fanny found the couple entrancing and was particularly interested in Sir George's stories of local beliefs and superstitions. The Musgraves returned her liking and very soon she and Thomas Adolphus were frequent visitors at Edenhall. One evening, however, an incident occurred which might have warned Fanny that Sir George was an awkward man to cross. It so happened that at dinner Thomas Adolphus was seated next to a very pretty girl and afterwards, anxious to rejoin her in the drawing-room and growing impatient at the length of time the older men were taking over their port, he made some excuse to leave the dining-room. Before he reached the door his host roared at him, "Come back! We won't have any of your damned forineering habits here! Come back and stick to your wine, or by the Lord I'll have the door locked!"

Fanny found the story highly amusing at the time—a little later she was not so sure. It was late autumn before she and Thomas Anthony were settled into Carlton Hill, some delay having been caused by the fact that there was a considerable drop between the lower edge of the field and the road which ran below. Since it was absolutely necessary to have a proper carriage entrance a good deal of building up had to be done before a drive could be constructed, and in course of this work the stream flowing from a little spring in the roadside bank had to be diverted. Nobody thought anything of the incident until Sir George and Lady Musgrave paid their first visit to the house. Fanny, gaily entertaining other guests in the drawing-room, heard a strange commotion in the hall. Suddenly the door burst open and a purple-faced Sir George strode in. "Woman!" he roared, "you've moved a holy well! That means you'll not live here for long!"

His tone implied she wouldn't live anywhere for very long, but at the time Fanny was not seriously disturbed. Only as the winter deepened, and the winds screeched and howled round Carlton Hill, and the snowdrifts piled up round her delicate flowering trees did she begin to feel there might be something in the ridiculous superstition after all. Besides, while the Musgraves were still outwardly polite they no longer treated the Trollopes as intimates—and Fanny soon discovered that there were few other families in the neighbourhood with whom she cared to make friends.

The matriarchal mood was on the wane—and it sank further into eclipse in January 1843 when Anthony came to stay. Eighteen months or so earlier he had, greatly to Fanny's wrath, left the secretary's office at St. Martin's-le-Grand to take up a post which nobody else wanted, that of Post Office surveyor at Banagher on the Shannon River in Ireland. In the short time he had spent there he had changed almost out of recognition. Shaggy in appearance, rough in manner he would always remain, but when he strode confidently into Carlton Hill his mother and brother blinked at him open-mouthed. Surely this big man with the genial laugh, the twinkling blue eyes, wasn't their Anthony? Straddled in his favourite position in front of the fire he regaled them with astonishing stories of Catholic priests, the hunting-field, renegade post-masters, and "leppers." "And what," said Fanny faintly, "may leppers be?"

Anthony gave his jovial ha-ha-ha! "Steeplechasers, Mama. I recollect only two months ago . . ." and off he went on another incredible story.

As she listened Fanny tried to pull her wits together. Her ugly duckling had matured with a vengeance, turned into a bluff country gentleman who smelt faintly of the stable and lived, so far as she could gather, on roast goose and whisky. She did not altogether approve of the transition and yet . . . for the first time she regarded her younger son with something akin to respect and when he clapped Thomas Adolphus on the shoulder and cried he must return with him to view the wonders of western Ireland she made no demur.

But the night before their departure she contrived to be left alone with Anthony. Was he really interested in his work, she asked, was he contented with this strange new life?

Yes, he told her gently and patted her hand. "Don't worry about me, Mama, I am truly happy—but you are not."

Fanny straightened defensively, but Anthony shook his head and went on, "You have grown so used to looking after us all that you can't stop. And you must. Why should you linger here when the world is yours to choose? Cecilia and John are perfectly capable of bringing up their child and remember"—here his singularly sweet smile flashed out— " 'the sun yoked his horses too far from Penrith town.' "

It was a phrase Fanny repeated to herself many times during Thomas Adolphus' absence and on his return in March, full of tales about Anthony's popularity, she said abruptly that she wanted to put the house up for sale. Bewildered but secretly relieved, he asked if she contemplated taking another in London. "No," said Fanny, "I want to sell all the furniture too. We can live in our boxes for a time. After all, we have 'the world before us where to choose' "; then her eyes filled with tears. "Stupid Anthony," she added softly, "he never could get a quotation right."

(*vii*)

They spent the summer with dear Fanny Bent, taking her to Ilfracombe for several weeks before returning to her Exeter home. There, walking on Northernhay in the shadowy autumn evenings, they discussed the question, "Where next?" They thought of Paris, of Dresden, Rome, Venice—but those, Fanny pointed out, were places to visit for a few months at a time and what she wanted—indeed, they both wanted, for they had many commissions to fulfil— was a place in which they could live comfortably but economically for two or three years, thus saving money for travelling about each summer. Practically simultaneously they exclaimed, Florence! They knew and liked the city, they had many friends there, it was supposed to be cheap to live in. Characteristically they wasted no time. They bade good-bye to Fanny Bent, and within a week were on their way to London. Equally characteristically Fanny suggested during the Channel crossing that they should make a little tour of Savoy first, since there was really no hurry to reach the city she always called *Firenze la gentile*.

As a rule Fanny's more impulsive actions turned out well but now she committed one which led to considerable unpleasantness later on. In Paris she had made friends with Lady (Rosina Lytton) Bulwer, that handsome, brilliant but definitely eccentric woman whose odd behaviour made her a host of enemies. Fanny had liked her, and had therefore championed her cause on many occasions. So soon as she had decided upon Florence as a possible home she had written to her friend, who had an apartment far too big for her in the Palazzo Passerini, to ask if she could accept Thomas Adolphus and herself as paying-guests. Lady Bulwer was overjoyed and when her dear Trollopes arrived in the October she greeted them in the most affectionate manner.

Alas, it was not long before her guests (especially Fanny) found that at close quarters their hostess possessed several traits which were not displayed in public. She had a vicious tongue—she annoyed Fanny by alluding to Mr. Colburn, the publisher, as "that embodied shiver"; she was a malicious scandal-monger; she had the devil's own temper; she was absolutely incapable of estimating the characters of her fellow-men and she was hopelessly extravagant.

Soon after the Trollope's arrival she complained of being in great pain. The efficient Fanny ministered to her but, alarmed by her bouts of weeping, she urged her to have a doctor. Lady Bulwer whirled on her in a fury. "How *can* you tell me to do any such thing, when you know that I have not a guinea for the purpose?" Still sympathetic, Fanny murmured that she must not worry, but just as she was about to send Thomas Adolphus for the medico a servant entered with a bill on a salver to announce that the silversmith was at the back door asking for his money. Lady Bulwer went into a fit of hysterics and handed the account to her startled guest who noted that it was for a pair of silver spurs and an ornamental silver collar ordered a week or two previously for the *ceremonial knighting of her little dog Taffy!* There were various similar exhibitions of hysterical rage, culminating in a dreadful scene during a picnic in the Boboli Gardens. Lady Bulwer herself arranged the expedition, laughingly reminding the other ladies that the climb to the gardens was a steep one. With much gallantry each gentleman gave his arm to a feminine companion, Lady Bulwer insisting that *Illustrissimo Signor Tommaso,* as she called Thomas Adolphus, should be her escort. The party were progressing slowly but surely when the air was rent with a noise like a train whistle and, looking round in amaze, they saw their hostess dash from the path, and throw herself flat on the turf. "It is TOO hot!" she screamed. "It is cruel to bring one here!"

This episode decided Fanny to seek new quarters without delay; but apartments in Florence were not nearly so easy to obtain as houses in London and they had to suffer several more of Lady Bulwer's tantrums before they found charming rooms in the Palazzo Berti, situated in the ominously named Via dei Malcontenti—once the road leading to the Florentine Tyburn. Here their peaceful, happy life in Florence really began and soon Fanny, as energetic and full of fun as ever, despite her sixty-three years, had drawn around her all that was brightest and best in Florentine society. Her Friday afternoon receptions were always crowded, her friends ranged from Lord Holland, the British Minister, to the ageing and pathetic Walter Savage Landor; and her appearance as Mrs. Malaprop in Arthur Vansittart's amateur production of *The Rivals* brought down the house.

There was no longer any question of regarding Florence as a temporary resting-place; it was home and neither Fanny nor Thomas Adolphus had the least wish to leave it. The days whirled by in a gay kaleidoscope—Grand-ducal parties at the Pitti Palace, a call from charming Charles Dickens (Fanny always insisted his eyes were hazel, not blue as Carlyle said), summer visits to the Baths at Lucca and winter visits to Rome, the arrival of Elizabeth Barrett and Robert Browning. . . . Ah, there was no end to the joy of Florentine life!

But Fanny had forgotten "Time's wingéd chariot," had forgotten too the grey mists of Lakeland in the winter and the cruel disease which had already claimed two of her children. Of course she thought a great deal about Cecilia and Anthony (who had married a seemingly pleasant girl called Rose Heseltine in 1844) and she wrote to them frequently, but in some odd way they had receded until they became doll-sized. . . . Then one day in the summer of 1847 when she was sitting in the garden she reflected dreamily how the years in *Firenze la gentile* had flown past.

Presently she heard footsteps and looked up to see Thomas Adolphus walking down the path towards her, a bundle of letters in his hand. The envelope on top of the pile bore Anthony's handwriting and as she slit it open she remarked jokingly that doutbless the epistle would contain four pages about horses and two lines about Rose—but she had read only the first paragraph when she gave a gasp and sat bolt-upright. "Anthony," she cried, "Anthony has written a novel!"

"Nonsense!" said Thomas Adolphus. "He can barely string two sentences together."

"Shush!" reproved Fanny, and read aloud, " 'The title is *The Macdermots of Ballycloran* and Mr. T. C. Newby of London is publishing it.' " She laid the letter in her lap and looked into the middle distance. "Just imagine," she whispered, "Anthony has written a novel!"

There were many qualities Thomas Adolphus admired in his brother, but intellect was not one of them. He was also a trifle chagrined that Anthony should dare, so to speak, poach on his preserves. "Newby!" he snorted. "Why, you know what they call him in London?—'the refuge of the destitute.' "

To his surprise his mother did not even smile: indeed, she scarcely heard him, so full of pride was her heart. So Anthony hadn't stayed a clerk after all; he had benefited from her example and from the years during which she had tried (Ah, how hard she had tried!) to coax him into the paths of learning. "I can scarcely wait to see the book," she murmured.

"It won't sell," said Thomas Adolphus, "nothing of Newby's ever sells." (He was right, but the fact remains that the despised Mr. Newby published in the same year as Anthony Trollope's first novel a book called *Wuthering Heights*.)

Fanny rose, scattering the remainder of her letters on the path. "I must write the boy at once," she said firmly, "and also recommend him to Mr. Bentley," and as she walked towards the house Anthony was no longer doll-size in her mind; instead he assumed the shape of a very large swan.

Alas, within a very few days her pleasure at Anthony's achievement was dimmed by an ominous letter from John Tilley. Cecilia had been far from well for some time past. He hadn't believed the local doctor's diagnosis of phthisis;

instead he had taken her to a first-class London specialist who had unfortunately confirmed the Penrith medico's verdict and said that her only hope was to winter in a warmer clime.

On the instant the gracious Mrs. Frances Trollope, friend of princes and diplomats, widely read author, famous Florentine hostess vanished; and in her place stood the indomitable woman who had sailed the Atlantic twenty years earlier. In a crisp voice she issued instructions to Thomas Adolphus: Cecilia must not come to Florence because of the treacherous winds which blew down from the Apennines. He must go forthwith to Rome and rent a roomy, sunny and quiet apartment. She would write to John telling him to bring Cecilia out as soon as possible and leave her in her mother's care.

Thomas Adolphus found a suitable apartment in a small *palazzo* in the Via delle Quattro Fontane and rather hesitantly asked his mother if she did not think that Miss Theodosia Garrow would be an excellent young companion for Cecilia—a remark which caused Fanny to smile for the first time in a week. Dear Thomas Adolphus, who imagined he was carefully concealing his growing affection for Miss Garrow, a delightful, highly intelligent girl who had come to reside in Florence with her parents several years before and was a close friend of Elizabeth Barrett Browning. Marriage with Theodosia would do nothing to disturb the perfect partnership; indeed Fanny welcomed the idea. She said hastily that she thought it an excellent notion for her to join them in Rome.

And Theodosia proved invaluable that winter, for she and Cecilia developed a deep affection for each other. They would talk for hours while Fanny wielded her grey goose quill, for the sixties had brought no slowing-down of her output and she still kept to the habit of writing so many words a day. But by Christmas it was evident that no change of climate was going to help Cecilia and for the third time Fanny had to tend a dying child, cheer her by recounting silly family jokes and reminiscences, assure her that in the spring all would be well. She played her part admirably, but occasionally even her courage faltered and it is noteworthy that that winter she developed the only morbid fear she had ever known—a dread of being buried alive. The law, she told Thomas Adolphus gravely, allowed far too short a time for a body to remain unburied after death; therefore she demanded his solemn promise that when she died he would cause a vein to be opened in her arm. Alarmed beyond measure at such words from his mother he gave the promise, but in his memoirs he told of the difficulty he had in making the physician carry it out.

Early in 1848 Fanny demanded point-blank why Thomas Adolphus was shilly-shallying over proposing to Theodosia. He replied that he had nothing to offer her but his small and precarious literary earnings, whereupon she explained to him with all her old vigour exactly how matters could be arranged. Old Mr. Garrow (his wife was lately dead) lived in Florence but would be only too pleased to move to less cramped quarters and, in addition, keep the ministrations of Theodosia. She herself loved her future daughter-in-law and had no fears about living under the same roof with her. All that Thomas Adolphus had to do was to find a house large enough to hold them all.

Nobody, least of all Thomas Adolphus, could stand up to Mama when she propounded one of her brilliant plans and a house on the corner of the Piazza dell Indipendenza was taken. How Fanny dealt with old Mr. Garrow's mumbled objections is not known, but eventually he agreed to both marriage and housing suggestion. On April 3, 1848, Thomas

The Perfect Partnership

Adolphus married his Theodosia in the British Minister's chapel in Florence and when he and his bride returned from their honeymoon Mr. Garrow was already settled in the newly named Villino Trollope.

After Cecilia's death Fanny joined them; but she was not, and was never to be again, quite the same Fanny as before.

Twilight in Tuscany
1848-1863

IT WOULD be entirely wrong to give the impression that Cecilia's death changed Fanny overnight into a feeble old woman. For several years she continued to write, to give and attend parties, to delight friends and acquaintances with sparkling conversation; but to those who had been close to her it seemed that her vivid personality was slightly dulled, rather in the way that the bright, rich pigments in an old painting become blurred with time. Her movements slowed down. No longer did she trit-trot briskly round house and garden; she walked slowly and as little as possible; and she began to suffer from deafness. (The Fanny of even 1846 would have found deafness intolerable: the Fanny of 1848 did not find the disability any trial.) She was gentler too in many ways, and people who met her for the first time disbelieved all the tales they had heard of her sharp wit.

She still found life fun. She chuckled all day when Thomas Adolphus translated for her a ridiculous, half-heard conversation he had held with Landor, who was also deaf. Landor had inquired after Fanny's health, and he had replied that she was very well but very deaf. "Dead, is she?" cried Landor, "I wish I were! I can't sleep, but I very soon shall, soundly too, and all the twenty-four hours round!"

But the glowing, vital, indomitable Fanny had gone and in her place was a sweet-faced old lady who sat in her drawing-room giving mechanical little nods and smiles in answer to questions she had not heard, or drove abroad in a pony chaise paying little attention to the scenes around her. Not that she was unhappy—far from that, for she had her treasure-store of memories into which to delve, and to her memories meant so much more than the present day—but those who loved and watched over her felt uneasy as they began to realise that her quick bright mind was going to perish long before her exceptionally wiry and healthy physical frame.

By the time her grandchild Bice was born, some four years after Theosodia and Thomas Adolphus's marriage, Fanny was beyond indulging in matriarchal moods. She loved the baby dearly but was content to leave all care of her to others and spend most of her days sitting either on the little terrace or by the window in her work-room. There were no more daily stints of work—indeed all too often the sentences traced by the grey goose quill were quite incomprehensible—and gradually, very gradually, memory of the immediate past faded. She couldn't remember whether that nice Mr. Lewes was the husband of Elizabeth Barrett or whether Robert Browning was married to the writer George Eliot, and nine times out of ten she addressed people she had known for years by the wrong name and laughed merrily when her son or daughter-in-law gently corrected the mistake. "Oh, dear!" she would say with a flash of the old vivacity, "and I *do* dislike stupidity so much!"

Before her eightieth birthday was reached her memory, according to Thomas Adolphus, had completely gone; but while it is undoubtedly true that she had absolutely no recollection of what had happened in recent years one cannot help but wonder if she dwelt in some inner world of the past. Could she otherwise have remained so philosophical, so serenely content with her lot? Or did kind nature, knowing all her tribulations, erase them utterly from her mind?

Certainly she never knew of her ugly duckling's literary triumphs (and how one regrets she did not), for when Thomas Adolphus told her that Anthony had gone to America she looked at him with a puzzled expression. "Anthony!" she echoed. "Who is Anthony and where, pray, is America?" But sometimes in the afternoons she would walk slowly to the bookcases which lined her room and pause before the two long shelves holding her own works. They were so pretty, so very pretty, and lovingly she would run her hand along their bindings. Whoever had managed to write them all, she thought, must have been a very clever person. . . .

But presently the powers of her mind disintegrated altogether and she was just a very old, senile woman—so far as anybody could judge. On the day she died Thomas Adolphus was sitting by her bedside. Suddenly he saw a change come over the face he adored. The deep-etched lines of age disappeared, the features became firm and strong again. Was she thinking, this woman of infinite courage, of the happy days in Keppel Street when she dreamed of Thomas Anthony enthroned on the Woolsack? He did not know, but as he watched her lips curved in a smile. "Cecilia!" she called, and her voice was clear as a bell. "Cecilia!"

Bibliography

Domestic Manners of the Americans. With illustrations by A. Hervieu. 2 vols. London. Whittaker, Treacher, 1832.

The Refugee in America: A Novel. 3 vols. London. Whittaker, Treacher. 1832.

The Mother's Manual: or Illustrations of Matrimonial Economy. An Essay in Verse. With illustrations by A. Hervieu. 1 vol. London. Treuttel and Wurtz and Richter. 1833.

The Abbess: A Romance. 3 vols. London. Whittaker, Treacher. 1833.

Belgium and Western Germany in 1833. 2 vols. London. John Murray. 1834.

Tremordyn Cliff. 3 vols. London. Bentley. 1835.

Paris and the Parisians in 1835. With illustrations by A. Hervieu. 2 vols. London. Bentley. 1836.

The Life and Adventures of Jonathan Jefferson Whitlaw: or Scenes on the Mississippi. With illustrations by A. Hervieu. 3 vols. London. Bentley. 1836. (Re-issued in 1857 under the title: *Lynch Law.*)

The Vicar of Wrexhill. With illustrations by A. Hervieu. 3 vols. London. Bentley. 1837.

Vienna and the Austrians. With illustrations by A. Hervieu. 2 vols. London. Bentley. 1838.

A Romance of Vienna. 3 vols. London. Bentley. 1838.

The Widow Barnaby. 3 vols. London. Bentley. 1839.

The Widow Married: a Sequel to The Widow Barnaby. With illustrations by R. W. Buss. 3 vols. London. Colburn. 1840.

The Life and Adventures of Michael Armstrong, the Factory Boy. With illustrations by A. Hervieu, R. W. Buss and T. Onwhyn. 3 vols. and 1 vol. (8vo). London. Colburn. 1840.

One Fault: A Novel. 3 vols. London. Bentley. 1840.

Charles Chesterfield: or the Adventures of a Youth of Genius. With illustrations by "Phiz." 3 vols. London. Colburn. 1841.

The Ward of Thorpe Combe. 3 vols. London. Bentley. 1841. (Re-issued in Ward, Lock's Parlour Library, and later as a Routledge Railway Novel under the title: *The Ward.*)

The Blue Bells of England. 3 vols. London. Saunders and Otley. 1842.

A Visit to Italy. 2 vols. London. Bentley. 1842.

The Barnabys in America: or Adventures of the Widow Wedded. With illustrations by John Leech. 3 vols. London. Colburn. 1843.

Hargrave: or the Adventures of a Man of Fashion. 3 vols. London. Colburn. 1843.

Jessie Phillips: A Tale of the Present Day. With illustrations by John Leech. 3 vols. London. Colburn. 1843. 1 vol. (8vo). 1844.

The Laurringtons: or Superior People. 3 vols. Longman, Brown, Green and Longmans. 1844.

Young Love: A Novel. 3 vols. Colburn. 1844.

The Attractive Man. 3 vols. London. Colburn. 1846.

The Robertses on their Travels. 3 vols. London. Colburn. 1846.

Travels and Travellers: A Series of Sketches. 2 vols. London. Colburn. 1846.

Father Eustace: A Tale of the Jesuits. 3 vols. London. Colburn. 1847.

The Three Cousins. 3 vols. London. Colburn. 1847.

Town and Country: A Novel. 3 vols. London. Colburn, 1848. (Re-issued in 1857 under the title: *Days of Regency*).

The Young Countess: or Love and Jealousy. 3 vols. London. Colburn. 1848. (Re-issued under the title: *Love and Jealousy* in Ward, Lock's Railway Library, and later by C. H. Clark.)

The Lottery of Marriage: A Novel. 3 vols. London. Colburn. 1849.

The Old World and the New: A Novel. 3 vols. London. Colburn. 1849.

Bibliography

Petticoat Government: A Novel. 3 vols. London. Colburn. 1850.

Mrs. Mathews, or Family Mysteries. 3 vols. London. Colburn. 1851.

Second Love, or Beauty and Intellect: A Novel. 3 vols. London. Colburn. 1851.

Uncle Walter: A Novel. 3 vols. London. Colburn. 1852.

The Young Heiress: A Novel. 3 vols. London. Hurst and Blackett. 1853

The Life and Adventures of a Clever Woman. Illustrated with Occasional Extracts from her Diary. 3 vols. London. Hurst and Blackett. 1854.

Gertrude: or Family Pride. 3 vols. London. Hurst and Blackett. 1855.

Fashionable Life: or Paris and London. 3 vols. London. Hurst and Blackett. 1856.

Index

Index

Index

Index

Index